on a more serious n
OUR COPYRIGHT NOTE

PUSH POWER BOSS JOURNAL + PLANNER

PUBLISHER
TA MEDIA & PRODUCTIONS LLC
DALLAS, TX 75240
www.PUBLISHYOURBOOKTODAY.INFO
WWW.TAMEDIACO.COM

let's get started
WHAT'S INSIDE
01

Reflect on 2021 to celebrate your big accomplishments and learn from your challenges. Set new 2022 intentions with actionable worksheets that will guide you to create achievable plans in your business. Plan out your days, weeks, and entire year with organized planners that will help you stay focused on what really matters. Set financial goals to help you grow your abundance mindset in your business.

let's get started
WHAT'S INSIDE
02

- QUOTE PAGE NOTE TO SELF (FILL-IN)
- DAILY INTENTION PAGES
- GRATITUDE JOURNAL PAGE
- PAST YEAR REFLECTION JOURNAL PAGES
- LOOKING FORWARD JOURNAL PAGES
- BLANK JOURNAL PAGES
- GOAL SETTING PAGES
- MONTHLY, WEEKLY,
- DAILY PLANNER PAGES
- PROJECT PLANNER PAGE
- FINANCIAL PLANNER
- PAGES
- HOLIDAYS
- 12 MONTHLY CALENDAR PAGES
- FILL-IN CALENDAR PAGE

bio

Cheronda Hester CEO of Push Power Boss. Her goal is to empower women in the areas of self-esteem, self-worth, and self-growth. By providing knowledge, direction, self-awareness through books, workshops, seminars, programs, one on one counseling, and mentorship. Developing women to add value to their present and futuristic spheres of influence. She is a true believer of Proverbs 27:17 "Iron Sharpens Iron"!

TRUE SUCCESS IS FOUND IN SEEKING GOD WITH OUR WHOLE HEART, MIND, SOUL, AND STRENGTH!!!!!

FEAR

HAS TWO MEANINGS,

FORGET EVERYTHING

AND RUN,

OR

FACE EVERYTHING

AND RISE,

THE CHOICE IS YOURS.

speaker, life coach, credit specialist

CHERONDA L. HESTER

CONNECT ACROSS ALL
SOCIAL MEDIA PLATFORMS
JOIN OUR EMAIL LIST AT
WWW.PUSHPOWERBOSS.COM

#pushpowerboss

quote of the year

ALWAYS

BELIEVE IN THE

IMPOSSIBLE

Cheronda Hester

PUSH *power* BOSS

NOTE TO SELF

dear. _____

YOU HAVE COME SO FAR THIS YEAR. LOOK AT ALL YOU'VE ACCOMPLISHED ALREADY. NEXT YEAR YOU WILL LOOK BACK & SEE YOU WERE _____ ALL ALONG. IN A YEAR YOU'LL BE _____ & _____ I'M SO VERY PROUD OF YOU.

love you always,

_____

SIGN YOUR NAME HERE

Dear Boss Moms,

 CONGRATULATIONS on taking your first step to planning and accomplishing your goals! Ladies, it's one thing to be a mom, another to be a wife, but it's a whole different thing trying to be a Boss Mom. Dealing with the normal hustle and bustle of being a mom, along with being an entrepreneur, is a whole different story. Working a nine to five and building a business is work on top of having to be a mom and a wife.

Do you feel the stress of trying to accomplish both? No worries! This planner will help you destroy the guilt, fear, and anxiety when desiring to be an amazing mom, successful entrepreneur, and for some an excellent wife. When you allow this planner and journal to be a tool in your life, you will find yourself being more confident, excited, passionate, and determined to be the Boss Mom you've always desired to be!!!

This planner and journal is designed to help you with daily prioritizing. By prioritizing each day, you will discover that "finding balance" can be challenging for Boss Moms. However, we must prioritize because our lives can be full of surprises. Every day is different because our lives are impacted by multiple schedules. We often find that balancing doesn't always work and as a result, we end each day in frustration. Using the tools provided in this planner and journal helped me to become a very successful Boss Mom of seven, an amazing wife, a great daughter, a successful entrepreneur, an effective senior leader, and coach.

LADIES! ARE YOU READY FOR AN EPIC SHIFT THAT WILL NOT CAUSE YOU TO SACRIFICE BEING A MOM, WIFE, DAUGHTER, OR AN ENTREPRENEUR? Well, this planner and journal is just for you! Allow me to welcome you to the Boss Mom family. Get ready because... **BIG DREAMS DO COME TRUE!!**

Signed,

Cheronda L. Hester

CHERONDA L. HESTER

monthly intentions

MONTH OF:

_____

OPEN PROJECTS

_____
_____
_____
_____
_____
_____
_____
_____
_____

affirmations
I AM

MONTHLY INTENTIONS

01: _____
_____

02: _____
_____

03: _____
_____

04: _____
_____

05: _____
_____

06: _____
_____

07: _____
_____

weekly priorities

WEEK OF:

_____

MONDAY		DAILY FOCUS
_____		*monday*
_____		
_____		
TUESDAY		*tuesday*
_____		
_____		
WEDNESDAY		*wednesday*
_____		
_____		
_____		*thursday*
THURSDAY		
_____		
_____		*friday*
_____		
FRIDAY		
_____		*saturday*
_____		
_____		*sunday*
SAT / SUN		
_____		
_____		
_____		

DECIDE
COMMIT
SUCCEED

today's intentions

TODAY'S DATE:

TODAY'S TOP 3 INTENTIONS
01:
02:
03:

let's do this

_____
_____
_____
_____
_____
_____
_____
_____
_____
_____
_____

today's affirmations

I AM

DAILY WATER TRACKER

HABIT TRACKER							
	M	T	W	T	F	S	S
	M	T	W	T	F	S	S
	M	T	W	T	F	S	S

today's intentions

TODAY'S DATE:

_____

CALLS / EMAILS	HABIT TRACKER	DEADLINES

CALLS / EMAILS
_____
_____
_____
_____
_____
_____
_____

DEADLINES
_____
_____
_____
_____
_____
_____
_____

TODAY I AM THANKFUL FOR
01:
02:
03:

today's to do

_____   _____
_____   _____
_____   _____
_____   _____
_____   _____
_____   _____

FAITH WITHOUT WORK IS DEAD

gratitude reflection

GRATITUDE LIST:

01:
_____

_____

02:
_____

_____

03:
_____

_____

04:
_____

_____

05:
_____

_____

06:
_____

_____

07:
_____

_____

08:
_____

_____

09:
_____

_____

10:
_____

_____

11:
_____

_____

PEOPLE I'M THANKFUL FOR:

01:
_____

02:
_____

03:
_____

04:
_____

05:
_____

favorite memories

past year reflections

WHAT MOTIVATED YOU?   YOUR BIGGEST STRUGGLE?

TOP 3 ACCOMPLISHMENTS MADE THIS YEAR
01:
02:
03:

3 LESSONS LEARNED	3 THINGS YOU CREATED
01:	01:
02:	02:
03:	03:

WHAT WILL YOU TAKE WITH YOU IN 2022 & WHAT WILL YOU LEAVE BEHIND?

MAKE THINGS HAPPEN

past year reflections

DESCRIBE YOUR PAST YEAR IN ONE WORD

BIGGEST WINS OF THE YEAR
01:
02:
03:

BIGGEST CHALLENGES
01:
02:
03:

LESSONS LEARNED FROM WINS

01:
_____

02:
_____

03:

FROM CHALLENGES

01:
_____

02:
_____

03:

PEOPLE WHO SUPPORTED YOU THIS YEAR:

when you are finished, be sure to let these people know what they mean to you

Leadership
is based
On Inspiration,
Not Domination.
On Cooperation,
Not Intimidation.

looking forward

BRAINSTORM 10 WORDS THAT YOU WANT TO EMBODY 2022

3 SMALL MANIFESTATIONS
01:
02:
03:

3 BIG MANIFESTATIONS
01:
02:
03:

4 WAYS YOU WILL PUSH PAST YOUR COMFORT ZONE THIS YEAR

01:

02:

03:

04:

PICK ONE WORD FROM ABOVE TO EMBODY 2022

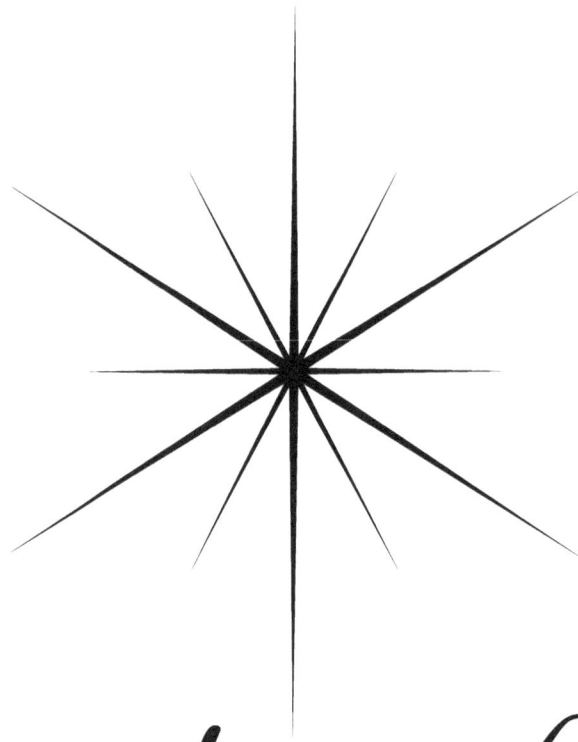

your abundance
is in
your faith

abundance journal

5 WORDS THAT DESCRIBE CURRENT BELIEFS TOWARDS MONEY

MONEY MANIFESTATIONS
01:
02:
03:
04:
05:
06:
07:

NEW OPPORTUNITIES TO
MANIFEST MORE ABUNDANCE

MY ABUNDANCE MINDSET
ALLOWS ME TO...

CURRENT RELATIONSHIP TO
ABUNDANCE IN MY BUSINESS

ABUNDANCE AFFIRMATIONS
I AM

BRILLIANT *thoughts*

BRILLIANT *thoughts*

BRILLIANT *thoughts*

_____
_____
_____
_____
_____
_____
_____
_____
_____
_____
_____
_____
_____
_____
_____
_____
_____
_____
_____
_____
_____
_____
_____
_____

IF **YOU** CAN'T STOP **THINKING ABOUT** IT, DON'T **STOP WOR**KING FOR **IT.**

BRILLIANT *thoughts*

_____
_____
_____
_____
_____
_____
_____
_____
_____
_____
_____
_____
_____
_____
_____
_____
_____
_____
_____
_____
_____
_____
_____
_____
_____

BRILLIANT *thoughts*

_____
_____
_____
_____
_____
_____
_____
_____
_____
_____
_____
_____
_____
_____
_____
_____
_____
_____
_____
_____
_____

BRILLIANT *thoughts*

_____
_____
_____
_____
_____
_____
_____
_____
_____
_____
_____
_____
_____
_____
_____
_____
_____
_____
_____
_____
_____
_____
_____
_____
_____
_____
_____
_____

BRILLIANT *thoughts*

_____
_____
_____
_____
_____
_____
_____
_____
_____
_____
_____
_____
_____
_____
_____
_____
_____
_____
_____
_____
_____
_____
_____
_____
_____
_____
_____

BRILLIANT *thoughts*

_____
_____
_____
_____
_____
_____
_____
_____
_____
_____
_____
_____
_____
_____
_____
_____
_____
_____
_____
_____
_____
_____
_____
_____
_____

BRILLIANT *thoughts*

PUSH
THROUGH

BRILLIANT *thoughts*

BRILLIANT *thoughts*

_____
_____
_____
_____
_____
_____
_____
_____
_____
_____
_____
_____
_____
_____
_____
_____
_____
_____
_____
_____
_____
_____
_____
_____
_____

BRILLIANT *thoughts*

BRILLIANT *thoughts*

BRILLIANT *thoughts*

_____
_____
_____
_____
_____
_____
_____
_____
_____
_____
_____
_____
_____
_____
_____
_____
_____
_____
_____
_____
_____
_____
_____
_____
_____

BRILLIANT *thoughts*

_____
_____
_____
_____
_____
_____
_____
_____
_____
_____
_____
_____
_____
_____
_____
_____
_____
_____
_____
_____
_____
_____
_____
_____

BRILLIANT *thoughts*

BRILLIANT *thoughts*

_____
_____
_____
_____
_____
_____
_____
_____
_____
_____
_____
_____
_____
_____
_____
_____
_____
_____
_____
_____
_____
_____
_____
_____

Acting on even a twig of faith Allows God to to grow it.

BRILLIANT *thoughts*

_____
_____
_____
_____
_____
_____
_____
_____
_____
_____
_____
_____
_____
_____
_____
_____
_____
_____
_____
_____
_____
_____
_____
_____
_____
_____
_____
_____

BRILLIANT *thoughts*

_____
_____
_____
_____
_____
_____
_____
_____
_____
_____
_____
_____
_____
_____
_____
_____
_____
_____
_____
_____
_____
_____
_____
_____
_____

BRILLIANT *thoughts*

_____
_____
_____
_____
_____
_____
_____
_____
_____
_____
_____
_____
_____
_____
_____
_____
_____
_____
_____
_____
_____
_____
_____
_____
_____

WEEKLY GOALS *week of*

MONDAY GOAL

TUESDAY GOAL

WEDNESDAY GOAL

ACTIONS STEPS

_____
_____
_____
_____
_____
_____
_____

ACTIONS STEPS

_____
_____
_____
_____
_____
_____
_____

ACTIONS STEPS

_____
_____
_____
_____
_____
_____
_____

THURSDAY GOAL

FRIDAY GOAL

SAT/SUN GOAL

ACTIONS STEPS

_____
_____
_____
_____
_____
_____

ACTIONS STEPS

_____
_____
_____
_____
_____
_____

ACTIONS STEPS

_____
_____
_____
_____
_____
_____

"

WHEN YOU'RE OVERWHELMED REMEMBER WHY YOU ARE DOING IT

this year's intentions

WORD OF THE YEAR:

_____

BUSINESS INTENTIONS:

ACTION STEPS:

01

02

03

04

FINANCIAL INTENTIONS:

ACTION STEPS:

01

02

03

04

GROWTH INTENTIONS:

ACTION STEPS:

01

02

03

04

BUSINESS GOALS *today's date:*

NEW PROJECTS:

_____
_____
_____
_____
_____
_____
_____
_____
_____

NEW CLIENTS:

_____
_____
_____
_____
_____
_____
_____
_____
_____

FINANCIAL:

_____
_____
_____
_____
_____
_____
_____
_____
_____

SOCIAL MEDIA:

_____
_____
_____
_____
_____
_____
_____
_____

MARKETING:

_____
_____
_____
_____
_____
_____
_____
_____

MINDSET:

_____
_____
_____
_____
_____
_____
_____
_____

I AM OPEN TO THE BEST THINGS IN LIFE

goal setting planner

START DATE:

_____

DEADLINE:

_____

MY BRILLIANT GOAL:

MY BIG WHY BEHIND THIS:

GOAL ACTION STEPS:	DEADLINE:
01:	
02:	
03:	
04:	
05:	
06:	
07:	
08:	
09:	

goal setting planner

START DATE: _____   DEADLINE: _____

MY BRILLIANT GOAL:

MY BIG WHY BEHIND THIS:

GOAL ACTION STEPS:	DEADLINE:
01:	
02:	
03:	
04:	
05:	
06:	
07:	
08:	
09:	

THE BEST THING IS **TO BELIEVE IN** YOURSELF

DAY PLANNER *today's date:*

WEEKLY PLANNER

morning   afternoon   evening

WIFE
MOM
BOSS

YEARLY PLANNER
write out your goals, intentions & plans

JAN

FEB

MAR

APR

MAY

JUN

JUL

AUG

SEP

OCT

NOV

DEC

PROJECT PLANNER

name of project:

MON	TUE	WED	THU	FRI	SAT	SUN

PROJECT PLANNER *name of project:*

MON	TUE	WED	THU	FRI	SAT	SUN

GO WHERE YOU *Feel* MOST alive

PROJECT PLANNER *name of project:*

MON	TUE	WED	THU	FRI	SAT	SUN

PROJECT PLANNER

name of project:

MON	TUE	WED	THU	FRI	SAT	SUN

PROJECT PLANNER

name of project:

MON	TUE	WED	THU	FRI	SAT	SUN

PROJECT PLANNER

name of project:

MON	TUE	WED	THU	FRI	SAT	SUN

SALE GOALS & PROJECTIONS *month of:*

REVENUE GOAL:	
# OF SALES NEEDED:	

PRODUCT SOLD	QTY	AMOUNT

SALE LOCATION (ETSY, WEBSITE)	SALES TOTAL

FINAL INCOME:	
FINAL # OF SALES:	

INCOME & EXPENSES *yearly overview*

MONTH	EXPENSES	INCOME	TOTAL
JAN			
FEB			
MAR			
APR			
MAY			
JUN			
JUL			
AUG			
SEP			
OCT			
NOV			
DEC			

TOTAL NET INCOME: _____

INCOME & EXPENSES *monthly breakdown*

INCOME GOAL:	
SAVINGS GOAL:	

GROSS MONTHLY INCOME	AMOUNT

BILLS & EXPENSES	AMOUNT	DUE

TOTAL INCOME	
TOTAL EXPENSES	
TOTAL PROFIT/LOSS	

HOLIDAYS & DAYS OFF *rest and recharge*

JAN 01
NEW YEARS DAY

FEB 15
PRESIDENT'S DAY

MAY 10
MOTHER'S DAY

SEP 06
LABOR DAY

JUNE 20
FATHER'S DAY

NOV 11
VETERN'S DAY

NOV 25
THANKSGIVING

JUL 04
INDEPENDENCE DAY

DEC 24
CHRISTMAS EVE

DEC 25
CHRISTMAS DAY

MAY 31
MEMORIAL DAY

MAR 23
BIRTHDAY

2022 MONTHLY CALENDAR

2022

JANUARY

SUN	MON	TUE	WED	THU	FRI	SAT
						1
2	3	4	5	6	7	8
9	10	11	12	13	14	15
16	17	18	19	20	21	22
23	24	25	26	27	28	29
30	31					

2022
FEBRUARY

SUN	MON	TUE	WED	THU	FRI	SAT
		1	2	3	4	5
6	7	8	9	10	11	12
13	14	15	16	17	18	19
20	21	22	23	24	25	26
27	28					

2022
MARCH

SUN	MON	TUE	WED	THU	FRI	SAT
		1	2	3	4	5
6	7	8	9	10	11	12
13	14	15	16	17	18	19
20	21	22	23	24	25	26
27	28	29	30	31		

2022
APRIL

SUN	MON	TUE	WED	THU	FRI	SAT
					1	2
3	4	5	6	7	8	9
10	11	12	13	14	15	16
17	18	19	20	21	22	23
24	25	26	27	28	29	30

SUN	MON	TUE	WED	THU	FRI	SAT
1	2	3	4	5	6	7
8	9	10	11	12	13	14
15	16	17	18	19	20	21
22	23	24	25	26	27	28
29	30	31				

JUNE

SUN	MON	TUE	WED	THU	FRI	SAT
			1	2	3	4
5	6	7	8	9	10	11
12	13	14	15	16	17	18
19	20	21	22	23	24	25
26	27	28	29	30		

2022
JULY

SUN	MON	TUE	WED	THU	FRI	SAT
					1	2
3	4	5	6	7	8	9
10	11	12	13	14	15	16
17	18	19	20	21	22	23
24	25	26	27	28	29	30
31						

SUN	MON	TUE	WED	THU	FRI	SAT
	1	2	3	4	5	6
7	8	9	10	11	12	13
14	15	16	17	18	19	20
21	22	23	24	25	26	27
28	29	30	31			

2022
SEPTEMBER

SUN	MON	TUE	WED	THU	FRI	SAT
				1	2	3
4	5	6	7	8	9	10
11	12	13	14	15	16	17
18	19	20	21	22	23	24
25	26	27	28	29	30	

SUN	MON	TUE	WED	THU	FRI	SAT
						1
2	3	4	5	6	7	8
9	10	11	12	13	14	15
16	17	18	19	20	21	22
23	24	25	26	27	28	29
30	31					

2022
NOVEMBER

SUN	MON	TUE	WED	THU	FRI	SAT
		1	2	3	4	5
6	7	8	9	10	11	12
13	14	15	16	17	18	19
20	21	22	23	24	25	26
27	28	29	30			

DECEMBER

SUN	MON	TUE	WED	THU	FRI	SAT
				1	2	3
4	5	6	7	8	9	10
11	12	13	14	15	16	17
18	19	20	21	22	23	24
25	26	27	28	29	30	31

2022

DAILY PLANNER

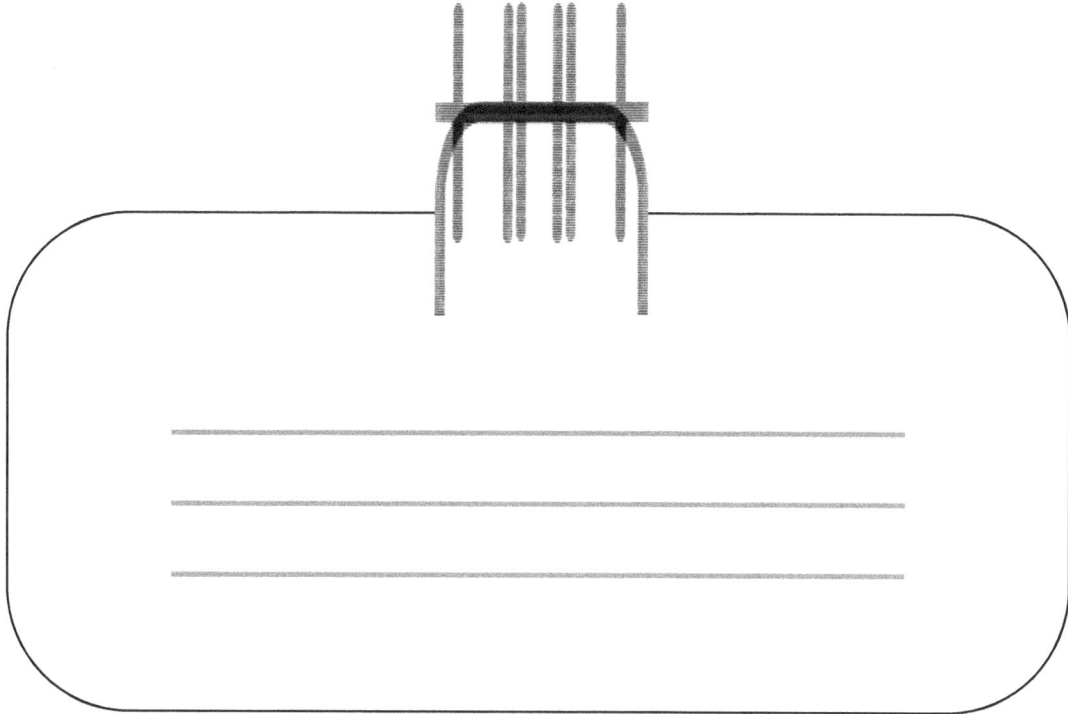

DAILY PLANNER

TODAY IS /

WEATHER

TODAY I AM EXCITED ABOUT

TODAY I AM GRATEFUL FOR

TODAY'S TOP PRIORITY

1. _____
2. _____
3. _____

TO DO LIST

_____
_____
_____
_____
_____
_____
_____
_____
_____
_____

TODAY'S SCHEDULE

PLAN		TRACK
_____	5.AM	_____
_____	6.AM	_____
_____	7.AM	_____
_____	8.AM	_____
_____	9.AM	_____
_____	10.AM	_____
_____	11.AM	_____
_____	12.PM	_____
_____	1.PM	_____
_____	3.PM	_____
_____	4.PM	_____
_____	5.PM	_____
_____	6.PM	_____
_____	7.PM	_____
_____	8.PM	_____
_____	9.PM	_____
_____	10.PM	_____
_____	11.PM	_____
_____	12.AM	_____

BREAKFAST

LUNCH

DINNER

WATER

HAPPY SCALE

MY REWARD

DAILY PLANNER

TODAY IS /

WEATHER

TODAY I AM EXCITED ABOUT

TODAY I AM GRATEFUL FOR

TODAY'S TOP PRIORITY

1.
2.
3.

TO DO LIST

TODAY'S SCHEDULE

PLAN		TRACK
	5.AM	
	6.AM	
	7.AM	
	8.AM	
	9.AM	
	10.AM	
	11.AM	
	12.PM	
	1.PM	
	3.PM	
	4.PM	
	5.PM	
	6.PM	
	7.PM	
	8.PM	
	9.PM	
	10.PM	
	11.PM	
	12.AM	

BREAKFAST

LUNCH

DINNER

WATER

HAPPY SCALE

MY REWARD

DAILY PLANNER

TODAY IS /

WEATHER

TODAY I AM EXCITED ABOUT

TODAY I AM GRATEFUL FOR

TODAY'S TOP PRIORITY

1. _____
2. _____
3. _____

TO DO LIST

_____
_____
_____
_____
_____
_____
_____
_____
_____
_____
_____

TODAY'S SCHEDULE

PLAN		TRACK
_____	5.AM	_____
_____	6.AM	_____
_____	7.AM	_____
_____	8.AM	_____
_____	9.AM	_____
_____	10.AM	_____
_____	11.AM	_____
_____	12.PM	_____
_____	1.PM	_____
_____	3.PM	_____
_____	4.PM	_____
_____	5.PM	_____
_____	6.PM	_____
_____	7.PM	_____
_____	8.PM	_____
_____	9.PM	_____
_____	10.PM	_____
_____	11.PM	_____
_____	12.AM	_____

BREAKFAST

LUNCH

DINNER

WATER

HAPPY SCALE

MY REWARD

DAILY PLANNER

TODAY IS /   WEATHER

TODAY I AM EXCITED ABOUT

TODAY I AM GRATEFUL FOR

TODAY'S TOP PRIORITY

1. _____
2. _____
3. _____

TO DO LIST

TODAY'S SCHEDULE

PLAN		TRACK
_____	5.AM	_____
_____	6.AM	_____
_____	7.AM	_____
_____	8.AM	_____
_____	9.AM	_____
_____	10.AM	_____
_____	11.AM	_____
_____	12.PM	_____
_____	1.PM	_____
_____	3.PM	_____
_____	4.PM	_____
_____	5.PM	_____
_____	6.PM	_____
_____	7.PM	_____
_____	8.PM	_____
_____	9.PM	_____
_____	10.PM	_____
_____	11.PM	_____
_____	12.AM	

BREAKFAST

LUNCH

DINNER

WATER

HAPPY SCALE

😃 🙂 😐 🙁 ☹️

MY REWARD

DAILY PLANNER

TODAY IS /   WEATHER

TODAY I AM EXCITED ABOUT

TODAY I AM GRATEFUL FOR

TODAY'S TOP PRIORITY

1. _____
2. _____
3. _____

TO DO LIST

TODAY'S SCHEDULE

PLAN		TRACK
_____	5.AM	_____
_____	6.AM	_____
_____	7.AM	_____
_____	8.AM	_____
_____	9.AM	_____
_____	10.AM	_____
_____	11.AM	_____
_____	12.PM	_____
_____	1.PM	_____
_____	3.PM	_____
_____	4.PM	_____
_____	5.PM	_____
_____	6.PM	_____
_____	7.PM	_____
_____	8.PM	_____
_____	9.PM	_____
_____	10.PM	_____
_____	11.PM	_____
_____	12.AM	_____

BREAKFAST   LUNCH

DINNER   WATER

HAPPY SCALE

😀   🙂   😐   🙁   😩

MY REWARD

DAILY PLANNER

TODAY IS /   WEATHER ☀ ⛅ 🌧 🌬 ❄

TODAY I AM EXCITED ABOUT

TODAY I AM GRATEFUL FOR

TODAY'S TOP PRIORITY

1. _____
2. _____
3. _____

TO DO LIST

_____
_____
_____
_____
_____
_____
_____
_____
_____
_____
_____
_____

TODAY'S SCHEDULE

PLAN		TRACK
_____	5.AM	_____
_____	6.AM	_____
_____	7.AM	_____
_____	8.AM	_____
_____	9.AM	_____
_____	10.AM	_____
_____	11.AM	_____
_____	12.PM	_____
_____	1.PM	_____
_____	3.PM	_____
_____	4.PM	_____
_____	5.PM	_____
_____	6.PM	_____
_____	7.PM	_____
_____	8.PM	_____
_____	9.PM	_____
_____	10.PM	_____
_____	11.PM	_____
_____	12.AM	

BREAKFAST

LUNCH

DINNER

WATER
🥛 🥛 🥛 🥛 🥛
🥛 🥛 🥛 🥛 🥛

HAPPY SCALE

😃 🙂 😐 🙁 😫

MY REWARD

DAILY PLANNER

TODAY IS /   WEATHER

TODAY I AM EXCITED ABOUT

TODAY I AM GRATEFUL FOR

TODAY'S TOP PRIORITY

1. _____
2. _____
3. _____

TO DO LIST

TODAY'S SCHEDULE

PLAN		TRACK
_____	5.AM	_____
_____	6.AM	_____
_____	7.AM	_____
_____	8.AM	_____
_____	9.AM	_____
_____	10.AM	_____
_____	11.AM	_____
_____	12.PM	_____
_____	1.PM	_____
_____	3.PM	_____
_____	4.PM	_____
_____	5.PM	_____
_____	6.PM	_____
_____	7.PM	_____
_____	8.PM	_____
_____	9.PM	_____
_____	10.PM	_____
_____	11.PM	_____
_____	12.AM	

BREAKFAST   LUNCH

DINNER   WATER

HAPPY SCALE

MY REWARD

DAILY PLANNER

TODAY IS /

WEATHER

TODAY I AM EXCITED ABOUT

TODAY I AM GRATEFUL FOR

TODAY'S TOP PRIORITY

1.

2.

3.

TO DO LIST

TODAY'S SCHEDULE

PLAN		TRACK
	5.AM	
	6.AM	
	7.AM	
	8.AM	
	9.AM	
	10.AM	
	11.AM	
	12.PM	
	1.PM	
	3.PM	
	4.PM	
	5.PM	
	6.PM	
	7.PM	
	8.PM	
	9.PM	
	10.PM	
	11.PM	
	12.AM	

BREAKFAST

LUNCH

DINNER

WATER

HAPPY SCALE

MY REWARD

DAILY PLANNER

TODAY IS /

WEATHER

TODAY I AM EXCITED ABOUT

TODAY I AM GRATEFUL FOR

TODAY'S TOP PRIORITY

1. _____
2. _____
3. _____

TO DO LIST

TODAY'S SCHEDULE

PLAN		TRACK
_____	5.AM	_____
_____	6.AM	_____
_____	7.AM	_____
_____	8.AM	_____
_____	9.AM	_____
_____	10.AM	_____
_____	11.AM	_____
_____	12.PM	_____
_____	1.PM	_____
_____	3.PM	_____
_____	4.PM	_____
_____	5.PM	_____
_____	6.PM	_____
_____	7.PM	_____
_____	8.PM	_____
_____	9.PM	_____
_____	10.PM	_____
_____	11.PM	_____
_____	12.AM	_____

BREAKFAST

LUNCH

DINNER

WATER

HAPPY SCALE

MY REWARD

DAILY PLANNER

TODAY IS /   WEATHER

TODAY I AM EXCITED ABOUT

TODAY I AM GRATEFUL FOR

TODAY'S TOP PRIORITY

1. _____
2. _____
3. _____

TO DO LIST

_____
_____
_____
_____
_____
_____
_____
_____
_____
_____
_____

TODAY'S SCHEDULE

PLAN		TRACK
_____	5.AM	_____
_____	6.AM	_____
_____	7.AM	_____
_____	8.AM	_____
_____	9.AM	_____
_____	10.AM	_____
_____	11.AM	_____
_____	12.PM	_____
_____	1.PM	_____
_____	3.PM	_____
_____	4.PM	_____
_____	5.PM	_____
_____	6.PM	_____
_____	7.PM	_____
_____	8.PM	_____
_____	9.PM	_____
_____	10.PM	_____
_____	11.PM	_____
_____	12.AM	_____

BREAKFAST

LUNCH

DINNER

WATER

HAPPY SCALE

MY REWARD

DAILY PLANNER

TODAY IS /

WEATHER

TODAY I AM EXCITED ABOUT

TODAY I AM GRATEFUL FOR

TODAY'S TOP PRIORITY

1. _____
2. _____
3. _____

TO DO LIST

_____
_____
_____
_____
_____
_____
_____
_____
_____
_____
_____

TODAY'S SCHEDULE

PLAN		TRACK
_____	5.AM	_____
_____	6.AM	_____
_____	7.AM	_____
_____	8.AM	_____
_____	9.AM	_____
_____	10.AM	_____
_____	11.AM	_____
_____	12.PM	_____
_____	1.PM	_____
_____	3.PM	_____
_____	4.PM	_____
_____	5.PM	_____
_____	6.PM	_____
_____	7.PM	_____
_____	8.PM	_____
_____	9.PM	_____
_____	10.PM	_____
_____	11.PM	_____
_____	12.AM	_____

BREAKFAST

LUNCH

DINNER

WATER

HAPPY SCALE

MY REWARD

DAILY PLANNER

📅 TODAY IS /

WEATHER

TODAY I AM EXCITED ABOUT

TODAY I AM GRATEFUL FOR

TODAY'S TOP PRIORITY

1. _____
2. _____
3. _____

TO DO LIST

_____
_____
_____
_____
_____
_____
_____
_____
_____

TODAY'S SCHEDULE

PLAN		TRACK
_____	5.AM	_____
_____	6.AM	_____
_____	7.AM	_____
_____	8.AM	_____
_____	9.AM	_____
_____	10.AM	_____
_____	11.AM	_____
_____	12.PM	_____
_____	1.PM	_____
_____	3.PM	_____
_____	4.PM	_____
_____	5.PM	_____
_____	6.PM	_____
_____	7.PM	_____
_____	8.PM	_____
_____	9.PM	_____
_____	10.PM	_____
_____	11.PM	_____
_____	12.AM	_____

BREAKFAST

LUNCH

DINNER

WATER

HAPPY SCALE

☺ ☺ 😐 ☹ ☹

MY REWARD

DAILY PLANNER

TODAY IS /

WEATHER

TODAY I AM EXCITED ABOUT

TODAY I AM GRATEFUL FOR

TODAY'S TOP PRIORITY

1. _____
2. _____
3. _____

TO DO LIST

TODAY'S SCHEDULE

PLAN		TRACK
_____	5.AM	_____
_____	6.AM	_____
_____	7.AM	_____
_____	8.AM	_____
_____	9.AM	_____
_____	10.AM	_____
_____	11.AM	_____
_____	12.PM	_____
_____	1.PM	_____
_____	3.PM	_____
_____	4.PM	_____
_____	5.PM	_____
_____	6.PM	_____
_____	7.PM	_____
_____	8.PM	_____
_____	9.PM	_____
_____	10.PM	_____
_____	11.PM	_____
_____	12.AM	_____

BREAKFAST

LUNCH

DINNER

WATER

HAPPY SCALE

MY REWARD

DAILY PLANNER

TODAY IS /

WEATHER

TODAY I AM EXCITED ABOUT

TODAY I AM GRATEFUL FOR

TODAY'S TOP PRIORITY

1.
2.
3.

TO DO LIST

TODAY'S SCHEDULE

PLAN		TRACK
	5.AM	
	6.AM	
	7.AM	
	8.AM	
	9.AM	
	10.AM	
	11.AM	
	12.PM	
	1.PM	
	3.PM	
	4.PM	
	5.PM	
	6.PM	
	7.PM	
	8.PM	
	9.PM	
	10.PM	
	11.PM	
	12.AM	

BREAKFAST

LUNCH

DINNER

WATER

HAPPY SCALE

😀 ☺ 😐 🙁 ☹

MY REWARD

DAILY PLANNER

TODAY IS /

WEATHER

TODAY I AM EXCITED ABOUT

TODAY I AM GRATEFUL FOR

TODAY'S TOP PRIORITY

1. _____
2. _____
3. _____

TO DO LIST

_____
_____
_____
_____
_____
_____
_____
_____
_____
_____

TODAY'S SCHEDULE

PLAN		TRACK
_____	5.AM	_____
_____	6.AM	_____
_____	7.AM	_____
_____	8.AM	_____
_____	9.AM	_____
_____	10.AM	_____
_____	11.AM	_____
_____	12.PM	_____
_____	1.PM	_____
_____	3.PM	_____
_____	4.PM	_____
_____	5.PM	_____
_____	6.PM	_____
_____	7.PM	_____
_____	8.PM	_____
_____	9.PM	_____
_____	10.PM	_____
_____	11.PM	_____
_____	12.AM	_____

BREAKFAST

LUNCH

DINNER

WATER

HAPPY SCALE

MY REWARD

DAILY PLANNER

📅 TODAY IS /

WEATHER

TODAY I AM EXCITED ABOUT

TODAY I AM GRATEFUL FOR

TODAY'S TOP PRIORITY

1. _____
2. _____
3. _____

TO DO LIST

_____
_____
_____
_____
_____
_____
_____
_____
_____
_____

TODAY'S SCHEDULE

PLAN		TRACK
_____	5.AM	_____
_____	6.AM	_____
_____	7.AM	_____
_____	8.AM	_____
_____	9.AM	_____
_____	10.AM	_____
_____	11.AM	_____
_____	12.PM	_____
_____	1.PM	_____
_____	3.PM	_____
_____	4.PM	_____
_____	5.PM	_____
_____	6.PM	_____
_____	7.PM	_____
_____	8.PM	_____
_____	9.PM	_____
_____	10.PM	_____
_____	11.PM	_____
_____	12.AM	_____

BREAKFAST

LUNCH

DINNER

WATER

HAPPY SCALE

😃 🙂 😐 🙁 ☹️

MY REWARD

DAILY PLANNER

📅 TODAY IS /

WEATHER

TODAY I AM EXCITED ABOUT

TODAY I AM GRATEFUL FOR

TODAY'S TOP PRIORITY

1. _____
2. _____
3. _____

TO DO LIST

TODAY'S SCHEDULE

PLAN		TRACK
_____	5.AM	_____
_____	6.AM	_____
_____	7.AM	_____
_____	8.AM	_____
_____	9.AM	_____
_____	10.AM	_____
_____	11.AM	_____
_____	12.PM	_____
_____	1.PM	_____
_____	3.PM	_____
_____	4.PM	_____
_____	5.PM	_____
_____	6.PM	_____
_____	7.PM	_____
_____	8.PM	_____
_____	9.PM	_____
_____	10.PM	_____
_____	11.PM	_____
_____	12.AM	_____

BREAKFAST   LUNCH

DINNER   WATER

HAPPY SCALE

😀 🙂 😐 🙁 😫

MY REWARD

DAILY PLANNER

TODAY IS /

WEATHER

TODAY I AM EXCITED ABOUT

TODAY I AM GRATEFUL FOR

TODAY'S TOP PRIORITY

1. _____
2. _____
3. _____

TO DO LIST

_____
_____
_____
_____
_____
_____
_____
_____
_____
_____
_____
_____
_____

TODAY'S SCHEDULE

PLAN		TRACK
_____	5.AM	_____
_____	6.AM	_____
_____	7.AM	_____
_____	8.AM	_____
_____	9.AM	_____
_____	10.AM	_____
_____	11.AM	_____
_____	12.PM	_____
_____	1.PM	_____
_____	3.PM	_____
_____	4.PM	_____
_____	5.PM	_____
_____	6.PM	_____
_____	7.PM	_____
_____	8.PM	_____
_____	9.PM	_____
_____	10.PM	_____
_____	11.PM	_____
_____	12.AM	_____

BREAKFAST

LUNCH

DINNER

WATER

HAPPY SCALE

MY REWARD

DAILY PLANNER

TODAY IS /

WEATHER

TODAY I AM EXCITED ABOUT

TODAY I AM GRATEFUL FOR

TODAY'S TOP PRIORITY

1. _____
2. _____
3. _____

TO DO LIST

TODAY'S SCHEDULE

PLAN		TRACK
_____	5.AM	_____
_____	6.AM	_____
_____	7.AM	_____
_____	8.AM	_____
_____	9.AM	_____
_____	10.AM	_____
_____	11.AM	_____
_____	12.PM	_____
_____	1.PM	_____
_____	3.PM	_____
_____	4.PM	_____
_____	5.PM	_____
_____	6.PM	_____
_____	7.PM	_____
_____	8.PM	_____
_____	9.PM	_____
_____	10.PM	_____
_____	11.PM	_____
_____	12.AM	_____

BREAKFAST

LUNCH

DINNER

WATER

HAPPY SCALE

MY REWARD

DAILY PLANNER

TODAY IS /

WEATHER

TODAY I AM EXCITED ABOUT

TODAY I AM GRATEFUL FOR

TODAY'S TOP PRIORITY

1.

2.

3.

TO DO LIST

TODAY'S SCHEDULE

PLAN		TRACK
	5.AM	
	6.AM	
	7.AM	
	8.AM	
	9.AM	
	10.AM	
	11.AM	
	12.PM	
	1.PM	
	3.PM	
	4.PM	
	5.PM	
	6.PM	
	7.PM	
	8.PM	
	9.PM	
	10.PM	
	11.PM	
	12.AM	

BREAKFAST

LUNCH

DINNER

WATER

HAPPY SCALE

MY REWARD

DAILY PLANNER

TODAY IS /

WEATHER

TODAY I AM EXCITED ABOUT

TODAY I AM GRATEFUL FOR

TODAY'S TOP PRIORITY

1. _____
2. _____
3. _____

TO DO LIST

_____
_____
_____
_____
_____
_____
_____
_____
_____
_____
_____
_____

TODAY'S SCHEDULE

PLAN		TRACK
_____	5.AM	_____
_____	6.AM	_____
_____	7.AM	_____
_____	8.AM	_____
_____	9.AM	_____
_____	10.AM	_____
_____	11.AM	_____
_____	12.PM	_____
_____	1.PM	_____
_____	3.PM	_____
_____	4.PM	_____
_____	5.PM	_____
_____	6.PM	_____
_____	7.PM	_____
_____	8.PM	_____
_____	9.PM	_____
_____	10.PM	_____
_____	11.PM	_____
_____	12.AM	_____

BREAKFAST

LUNCH

DINNER

WATER

HAPPY SCALE

MY REWARD

DAILY PLANNER

TODAY IS /

WEATHER

TODAY I AM EXCITED ABOUT

TODAY I AM GRATEFUL FOR

TODAY'S TOP PRIORITY

1. _____
2. _____
3. _____

TO DO LIST

_____
_____
_____
_____
_____
_____
_____
_____
_____
_____

TODAY'S SCHEDULE

PLAN		TRACK
_____	5.AM	_____
_____	6.AM	_____
_____	7.AM	_____
_____	8.AM	_____
_____	9.AM	_____
_____	10.AM	_____
_____	11.AM	_____
_____	12.PM	_____
_____	1.PM	_____
_____	3.PM	_____
_____	4.PM	_____
_____	5.PM	_____
_____	6.PM	_____
_____	7.PM	_____
_____	8.PM	_____
_____	9.PM	_____
_____	10.PM	_____
_____	11.PM	_____
_____	12.AM	_____

BREAKFAST

LUNCH

DINNER

WATER

HAPPY SCALE

MY REWARD

DAILY PLANNER

TODAY IS /

WEATHER

TODAY I AM EXCITED ABOUT

TODAY I AM GRATEFUL FOR

TODAY'S TOP PRIORITY

1. _____
2. _____
3. _____

TO DO LIST

_____
_____
_____
_____
_____
_____
_____
_____
_____
_____
_____

TODAY'S SCHEDULE

PLAN		TRACK
	5.AM	
	6.AM	
	7.AM	
	8.AM	
	9.AM	
	10.AM	
	11.AM	
	12.PM	
	1.PM	
	3.PM	
	4.PM	
	5.PM	
	6.PM	
	7.PM	
	8.PM	
	9.PM	
	10.PM	
	11.PM	
	12.AM	

BREAKFAST

LUNCH

DINNER

WATER

HAPPY SCALE

MY REWARD

DAILY PLANNER

📅 TODAY IS /

WEATHER

TODAY I AM EXCITED ABOUT

TODAY I AM GRATEFUL FOR

TODAY'S TOP PRIORITY

1. _____
2. _____
3. _____

TO DO LIST

_____
_____
_____
_____
_____
_____
_____
_____
_____
_____
_____

TODAY'S SCHEDULE

PLAN		TRACK
_____	5.AM	_____
_____	6.AM	_____
_____	7.AM	_____
_____	8.AM	_____
_____	9.AM	_____
_____	10.AM	_____
_____	11.AM	_____
_____	12.PM	_____
_____	1.PM	_____
_____	3.PM	_____
_____	4.PM	_____
_____	5.PM	_____
_____	6.PM	_____
_____	7.PM	_____
_____	8.PM	_____
_____	9.PM	_____
_____	10.PM	_____
_____	11.PM	_____
_____	12.AM	

BREAKFAST

LUNCH

DINNER

WATER

HAPPY SCALE

😄 🙂 😐 🙁 ☹️

MY REWARD

DAILY PLANNER

TODAY IS /

WEATHER

TODAY I AM EXCITED ABOUT

TODAY I AM GRATEFUL FOR

TODAY'S TOP PRIORITY

1. _____
2. _____
3. _____

TO DO LIST

_____
_____
_____
_____
_____
_____
_____
_____
_____
_____
_____

TODAY'S SCHEDULE

PLAN		TRACK
_____	5.AM	_____
_____	6.AM	_____
_____	7.AM	_____
_____	8.AM	_____
_____	9.AM	_____
_____	10.AM	_____
_____	11.AM	_____
_____	12.PM	_____
_____	1.PM	_____
_____	3.PM	_____
_____	4.PM	_____
_____	5.PM	_____
_____	6.PM	_____
_____	7.PM	_____
_____	8.PM	_____
_____	9.PM	_____
_____	10.PM	_____
_____	11.PM	_____
_____	12.AM	_____

BREAKFAST

LUNCH

DINNER

WATER

HAPPY SCALE

MY REWARD

DAILY PLANNER

TODAY IS /

WEATHER

TODAY I AM EXCITED ABOUT

TODAY I AM GRATEFUL FOR

TODAY'S TOP PRIORITY

1. _____
2. _____
3. _____

TO DO LIST

_____
_____
_____
_____
_____
_____
_____
_____
_____
_____
_____

TODAY'S SCHEDULE

PLAN		TRACK
_____	5.AM	_____
_____	6.AM	_____
_____	7.AM	_____
_____	8.AM	_____
_____	9.AM	_____
_____	10.AM	_____
_____	11.AM	_____
_____	12.PM	_____
_____	1.PM	_____
_____	3.PM	_____
_____	4.PM	_____
_____	5.PM	_____
_____	6.PM	_____
_____	7.PM	_____
_____	8.PM	_____
_____	9.PM	_____
_____	10.PM	_____
_____	11.PM	_____
_____	12.AM	

BREAKFAST

LUNCH

DINNER

WATER

HAPPY SCALE

MY REWARD

DAILY PLANNER

TODAY IS /

WEATHER

TODAY I AM EXCITED ABOUT

TODAY I AM GRATEFUL FOR

TODAY'S TOP PRIORITY

1. _____
2. _____
3. _____

TO DO LIST

_____
_____
_____
_____
_____
_____
_____
_____
_____
_____

TODAY'S SCHEDULE

PLAN		TRACK
_____	5.AM	_____
_____	6.AM	_____
_____	7.AM	_____
_____	8.AM	_____
_____	9.AM	_____
_____	10.AM	_____
_____	11.AM	_____
_____	12.PM	_____
_____	1.PM	_____
_____	3.PM	_____
_____	4.PM	_____
_____	5.PM	_____
_____	6.PM	_____
_____	7.PM	_____
_____	8.PM	_____
_____	9.PM	_____
_____	10.PM	_____
_____	11.PM	_____
_____	12.AM	_____

BREAKFAST

LUNCH

DINNER

WATER

HAPPY SCALE

MY REWARD

DAILY PLANNER

TODAY IS /

WEATHER

TODAY I AM EXCITED ABOUT

TODAY I AM GRATEFUL FOR

TODAY'S TOP PRIORITY

1. _____
2. _____
3. _____

TO DO LIST

_____
_____
_____
_____
_____
_____
_____
_____
_____
_____

TODAY'S SCHEDULE

PLAN		TRACK
_____	5.AM	_____
_____	6.AM	_____
_____	7.AM	_____
_____	8.AM	_____
_____	9.AM	_____
_____	10.AM	_____
_____	11.AM	_____
_____	12.PM	_____
_____	1.PM	_____
_____	3.PM	_____
_____	4.PM	_____
_____	5.PM	_____
_____	6.PM	_____
_____	7.PM	_____
_____	8.PM	_____
_____	9.PM	_____
_____	10.PM	_____
_____	11.PM	_____
_____	12.AM	_____

BREAKFAST

LUNCH

DINNER

WATER

HAPPY SCALE

MY REWARD

DAILY PLANNER

TODAY IS /   WEATHER

TODAY I AM EXCITED ABOUT

TODAY I AM GRATEFUL FOR

TODAY'S TOP PRIORITY

1. _____
2. _____
3. _____

TO DO LIST

_____
_____
_____
_____
_____
_____
_____
_____
_____
_____
_____

TODAY'S SCHEDULE

PLAN		TRACK
_____	5.AM	_____
_____	6.AM	_____
_____	7.AM	_____
_____	8.AM	_____
_____	9.AM	_____
_____	10.AM	_____
_____	11.AM	_____
_____	12.PM	_____
_____	1.PM	_____
_____	3.PM	_____
_____	4.PM	_____
_____	5.PM	_____
_____	6.PM	_____
_____	7.PM	_____
_____	8.PM	_____
_____	9.PM	_____
_____	10.PM	_____
_____	11.PM	_____
_____	12.AM	_____

BREAKFAST   LUNCH

DINNER   WATER

HAPPY SCALE

MY REWARD

DAILY PLANNER

TODAY IS /

WEATHER

TODAY I AM EXCITED ABOUT

TODAY I AM GRATEFUL FOR

TODAY'S TOP PRIORITY

1. _____
2. _____
3. _____

TO DO LIST

_____
_____
_____
_____
_____
_____
_____
_____
_____
_____
_____

TODAY'S SCHEDULE

PLAN		TRACK
_____	5.AM	_____
_____	6.AM	_____
_____	7.AM	_____
_____	8.AM	_____
_____	9.AM	_____
_____	10.AM	_____
_____	11.AM	_____
_____	12.PM	_____
_____	1.PM	_____
_____	3.PM	_____
_____	4.PM	_____
_____	5.PM	_____
_____	6.PM	_____
_____	7.PM	_____
_____	8.PM	_____
_____	9.PM	_____
_____	10.PM	_____
_____	11.PM	_____
_____	12.AM	_____

BREAKFAST

LUNCH

DINNER

WATER

HAPPY SCALE

MY REWARD

DAILY PLANNER

TODAY IS /   WEATHER

TODAY I AM EXCITED ABOUT

TODAY I AM GRATEFUL FOR

TODAY'S TOP PRIORITY

1. _____
2. _____
3. _____

TO DO LIST

_____
_____
_____
_____
_____
_____
_____
_____
_____
_____
_____

TODAY'S SCHEDULE

PLAN		TRACK
_____	5.AM	_____
_____	6.AM	_____
_____	7.AM	_____
_____	8.AM	_____
_____	9.AM	_____
_____	10.AM	_____
_____	11.AM	_____
_____	12.PM	_____
_____	1.PM	_____
_____	3.PM	_____
_____	4.PM	_____
_____	5.PM	_____
_____	6.PM	_____
_____	7.PM	_____
_____	8.PM	_____
_____	9.PM	_____
_____	10.PM	_____
_____	11.PM	_____
_____	12.AM	

BREAKFAST

LUNCH

DINNER

WATER

HAPPY SCALE

MY REWARD

DAILY PLANNER

TODAY IS /

WEATHER

TODAY I AM EXCITED ABOUT

TODAY I AM GRATEFUL FOR

TODAY'S TOP PRIORITY

1.

2.

3.

TO DO LIST

TODAY'S SCHEDULE

PLAN		TRACK
	5.AM	
	6.AM	
	7.AM	
	8.AM	
	9.AM	
	10.AM	
	11.AM	
	12.PM	
	1.PM	
	3.PM	
	4.PM	
	5.PM	
	6.PM	
	7.PM	
	8.PM	
	9.PM	
	10.PM	
	11.PM	
	12.AM	

BREAKFAST

LUNCH

DINNER

WATER

HAPPY SCALE

MY REWARD

DAILY PLANNER

📅 TODAY IS /

WEATHER

TODAY I AM EXCITED ABOUT

TODAY I AM GRATEFUL FOR

TODAY'S TOP PRIORITY

1. _____
2. _____
3. _____

TO DO LIST

_____
_____
_____
_____
_____
_____
_____
_____
_____
_____
_____
_____

TODAY'S SCHEDULE

PLAN		TRACK
_____	5.AM	_____
_____	6.AM	_____
_____	7.AM	_____
_____	8.AM	_____
_____	9.AM	_____
_____	10.AM	_____
_____	11.AM	_____
_____	12.PM	_____
_____	1.PM	_____
_____	3.PM	_____
_____	4.PM	_____
_____	5.PM	_____
_____	6.PM	_____
_____	7.PM	_____
_____	8.PM	_____
_____	9.PM	_____
_____	10.PM	_____
_____	11.PM	_____
_____	12.AM	_____

BREAKFAST

LUNCH

DINNER

WATER

HAPPY SCALE

😃 🙂 😐 🙁 ☹️

MY REWARD

DAILY PLANNER

📅 TODAY IS /

WEATHER

TODAY I AM EXCITED ABOUT

TODAY I AM GRATEFUL FOR

TODAY'S TOP PRIORITY

1. _____
2. _____
3. _____

TO DO LIST

_____
_____
_____
_____
_____
_____
_____
_____
_____
_____
_____

TODAY'S SCHEDULE

PLAN		TRACK
_____	5.AM	_____
_____	6.AM	_____
_____	7.AM	_____
_____	8.AM	_____
_____	9.AM	_____
_____	10.AM	_____
_____	11.AM	_____
_____	12.PM	_____
_____	1.PM	_____
_____	3.PM	_____
_____	4.PM	_____
_____	5.PM	_____
_____	6.PM	_____
_____	7.PM	_____
_____	8.PM	_____
_____	9.PM	_____
_____	10.PM	_____
_____	11.PM	_____
_____	12.AM	_____

BREAKFAST

LUNCH

DINNER

WATER

HAPPY SCALE

😃 ☺️ 😐 🙁 ☹️

MY REWARD

DAILY PLANNER

TODAY IS /

WEATHER

TODAY I AM EXCITED ABOUT

TODAY I AM GRATEFUL FOR

TODAY'S TOP PRIORITY

1. _____
2. _____
3. _____

TO DO LIST

_____
_____
_____
_____
_____
_____
_____
_____
_____
_____
_____

TODAY'S SCHEDULE

PLAN		TRACK
_____	5.AM	_____
_____	6.AM	_____
_____	7.AM	_____
_____	8.AM	_____
_____	9.AM	_____
_____	10.AM	_____
_____	11.AM	_____
_____	12.PM	_____
_____	1.PM	_____
_____	3.PM	_____
_____	4.PM	_____
_____	5.PM	_____
_____	6.PM	_____
_____	7.PM	_____
_____	8.PM	_____
_____	9.PM	_____
_____	10.PM	_____
_____	11.PM	_____
_____	12.AM	_____

BREAKFAST

LUNCH

DINNER

WATER

HAPPY SCALE

MY REWARD

DAILY PLANNER

TODAY IS /   WEATHER

TODAY I AM EXCITED ABOUT

TODAY I AM GRATEFUL FOR

TODAY'S TOP PRIORITY

1. _____
2. _____
3. _____

TO DO LIST

_____
_____
_____
_____
_____
_____
_____
_____
_____
_____
_____

TODAY'S SCHEDULE

PLAN		TRACK
_____	5.AM	_____
_____	6.AM	_____
_____	7.AM	_____
_____	8.AM	_____
_____	9.AM	_____
_____	10.AM	_____
_____	11.AM	_____
_____	12.PM	_____
_____	1.PM	_____
_____	3.PM	_____
_____	4.PM	_____
_____	5.PM	_____
_____	6.PM	_____
_____	7.PM	_____
_____	8.PM	_____
_____	9.PM	_____
_____	10.PM	_____
_____	11.PM	_____
_____	12.AM	_____

BREAKFAST   LUNCH

DINNER   WATER

HAPPY SCALE

MY REWARD

DAILY PLANNER

📅 TODAY IS /

WEATHER

TODAY I AM EXCITED ABOUT

TODAY I AM GRATEFUL FOR

TODAY'S TOP PRIORITY

1. _____
2. _____
3. _____

TO DO LIST

_____
_____
_____
_____
_____
_____
_____
_____
_____
_____
_____
_____

TODAY'S SCHEDULE

PLAN		TRACK
_____	5.AM	_____
_____	6.AM	_____
_____	7.AM	_____
_____	8.AM	_____
_____	9.AM	_____
_____	10.AM	_____
_____	11.AM	_____
_____	12.PM	_____
_____	1.PM	_____
_____	3.PM	_____
_____	4.PM	_____
_____	5.PM	_____
_____	6.PM	_____
_____	7.PM	_____
_____	8.PM	_____
_____	9.PM	_____
_____	10.PM	_____
_____	11.PM	_____
_____	12.AM	_____

BREAKFAST

LUNCH

DINNER

WATER

HAPPY SCALE

😀 🙂 😐 🙁 ☹️

MY REWARD

DAILY PLANNER

TODAY IS /

WEATHER

TODAY I AM EXCITED ABOUT

TODAY I AM GRATEFUL FOR

TODAY'S TOP PRIORITY

1.
2.
3.

TO DO LIST

TODAY'S SCHEDULE

PLAN		TRACK
	5.AM	
	6.AM	
	7.AM	
	8.AM	
	9.AM	
	10.AM	
	11.AM	
	12.PM	
	1.PM	
	3.PM	
	4.PM	
	5.PM	
	6.PM	
	7.PM	
	8.PM	
	9.PM	
	10.PM	
	11.PM	
	12.AM	

BREAKFAST

LUNCH

DINNER

WATER

HAPPY SCALE

MY REWARD

DAILY PLANNER

TODAY IS /

WEATHER

TODAY I AM EXCITED ABOUT

TODAY I AM GRATEFUL FOR

TODAY'S TOP PRIORITY

1. _____
2. _____
3. _____

TO DO LIST

_____
_____
_____
_____
_____
_____
_____
_____
_____
_____
_____
_____

TODAY'S SCHEDULE

PLAN		TRACK
_____	5.AM	_____
_____	6.AM	_____
_____	7.AM	_____
_____	8.AM	_____
_____	9.AM	_____
_____	10.AM	_____
_____	11.AM	_____
_____	12.PM	_____
_____	1.PM	_____
_____	3.PM	_____
_____	4.PM	_____
_____	5.PM	_____
_____	6.PM	_____
_____	7.PM	_____
_____	8.PM	_____
_____	9.PM	_____
_____	10.PM	_____
_____	11.PM	_____
_____	12.AM	

BREAKFAST

LUNCH

DINNER

WATER

HAPPY SCALE

MY REWARD

DAILY PLANNER

TODAY IS /   WEATHER ☀ ⛅ 🌧 🌬 ☀

TODAY I AM EXCITED ABOUT

TODAY I AM GRATEFUL FOR

TODAY'S TOP PRIORITY

1. _____
2. _____
3. _____

TO DO LIST

_____
_____
_____
_____
_____
_____
_____
_____
_____
_____
_____

TODAY'S SCHEDULE

PLAN		TRACK
_____	5.AM	_____
_____	6.AM	_____
_____	7.AM	_____
_____	8.AM	_____
_____	9.AM	_____
_____	10.AM	_____
_____	11.AM	_____
_____	12.PM	_____
_____	1.PM	_____
_____	3.PM	_____
_____	4.PM	_____
_____	5.PM	_____
_____	6.PM	_____
_____	7.PM	_____
_____	8.PM	_____
_____	9.PM	_____
_____	10.PM	_____
_____	11.PM	_____
_____	12.AM	

BREAKFAST	LUNCH

DINNER	WATER
	🥛 🥛 🥛 🥛 🥛 🥛 🥛 🥛 🥛 🥛

HAPPY SCALE

😀 🙂 😐 🙁 ☹

MY REWARD

DAILY PLANNER

TODAY IS /

WEATHER

TODAY I AM EXCITED ABOUT

TODAY I AM GRATEFUL FOR

TODAY'S TOP PRIORITY

1. _____
2. _____
3. _____

TO DO LIST

TODAY'S SCHEDULE

PLAN		TRACK
_____	5.AM	_____
_____	6.AM	_____
_____	7.AM	_____
_____	8.AM	_____
_____	9.AM	_____
_____	10.AM	_____
_____	11.AM	_____
_____	12.PM	_____
_____	1.PM	_____
_____	3.PM	_____
_____	4.PM	_____
_____	5.PM	_____
_____	6.PM	_____
_____	7.PM	_____
_____	8.PM	_____
_____	9.PM	_____
_____	10.PM	_____
_____	11.PM	_____
_____	12.AM	_____

BREAKFAST

LUNCH

DINNER

WATER

HAPPY SCALE

MY REWARD

DAILY PLANNER

📅 TODAY IS /

WEATHER

TODAY I AM EXCITED ABOUT

TODAY I AM GRATEFUL FOR

TODAY'S TOP PRIORITY

1. _____
2. _____
3. _____

TO DO LIST

_____
_____
_____
_____
_____
_____
_____
_____
_____
_____
_____

TODAY'S SCHEDULE

PLAN		TRACK
_____	5.AM	_____
_____	6.AM	_____
_____	7.AM	_____
_____	8.AM	_____
_____	9.AM	_____
_____	10.AM	_____
_____	11.AM	_____
_____	12.PM	_____
_____	1.PM	_____
_____	3.PM	_____
_____	4.PM	_____
_____	5.PM	_____
_____	6.PM	_____
_____	7.PM	_____
_____	8.PM	_____
_____	9.PM	_____
_____	10.PM	_____
_____	11.PM	_____
_____	12.AM	_____

BREAKFAST

LUNCH

DINNER

WATER

HAPPY SCALE

MY REWARD

DAILY PLANNER

TODAY IS /

WEATHER

TODAY I AM EXCITED ABOUT

TODAY I AM GRATEFUL FOR

TODAY'S TOP PRIORITY

1. _____
2. _____
3. _____

TO DO LIST

TODAY'S SCHEDULE

PLAN		TRACK
_____	5.AM	_____
_____	6.AM	_____
_____	7.AM	_____
_____	8.AM	_____
_____	9.AM	_____
_____	10.AM	_____
_____	11.AM	_____
_____	12.PM	_____
_____	1.PM	_____
_____	3.PM	_____
_____	4.PM	_____
_____	5.PM	_____
_____	6.PM	_____
_____	7.PM	_____
_____	8.PM	_____
_____	9.PM	_____
_____	10.PM	_____
_____	11.PM	_____
_____	12.AM	_____

BREAKFAST

LUNCH

DINNER

WATER

HAPPY SCALE

MY REWARD

DAILY PLANNER

📅 TODAY IS /

WEATHER

TODAY I AM EXCITED ABOUT

TODAY I AM GRATEFUL FOR

TODAY'S TOP PRIORITY

1. _____
2. _____
3. _____

TO DO LIST

_____
_____
_____
_____
_____
_____
_____
_____
_____
_____
_____

TODAY'S SCHEDULE

PLAN		TRACK
_____	5.AM	_____
_____	6.AM	_____
_____	7.AM	_____
_____	8.AM	_____
_____	9.AM	_____
_____	10.AM	_____
_____	11.AM	_____
_____	12.PM	_____
_____	1.PM	_____
_____	3.PM	_____
_____	4.PM	_____
_____	5.PM	_____
_____	6.PM	_____
_____	7.PM	_____
_____	8.PM	_____
_____	9.PM	_____
_____	10.PM	_____
_____	11.PM	_____
_____	12.AM	_____

BREAKFAST

LUNCH

DINNER

WATER

HAPPY SCALE

😀 🙂 😐 🙁 ☹️

MY REWARD

DAILY PLANNER

TODAY IS /   WEATHER

TODAY I AM EXCITED ABOUT

TODAY I AM GRATEFUL FOR

TODAY'S TOP PRIORITY

1. _____
2. _____
3. _____

TO DO LIST

_____
_____
_____
_____
_____
_____
_____
_____
_____
_____
_____

TODAY'S SCHEDULE

PLAN		TRACK
_____	5.AM	_____
_____	6.AM	_____
_____	7.AM	_____
_____	8.AM	_____
_____	9.AM	_____
_____	10.AM	_____
_____	11.AM	_____
_____	12.PM	_____
_____	1.PM	_____
_____	3.PM	_____
_____	4.PM	_____
_____	5.PM	_____
_____	6.PM	_____
_____	7.PM	_____
_____	8.PM	_____
_____	9.PM	_____
_____	10.PM	_____
_____	11.PM	_____
_____	12.AM	_____

BREAKFAST

LUNCH

DINNER

WATER

HAPPY SCALE

MY REWARD

DAILY PLANNER

TODAY IS /

WEATHER

TODAY I AM EXCITED ABOUT

TODAY I AM GRATEFUL FOR

TODAY'S TOP PRIORITY

1. _____
2. _____
3. _____

TO DO LIST

TODAY'S SCHEDULE

PLAN		TRACK
_____	5.AM	_____
_____	6.AM	_____
_____	7.AM	_____
_____	8.AM	_____
_____	9.AM	_____
_____	10.AM	_____
_____	11.AM	_____
_____	12.PM	_____
_____	1.PM	_____
_____	3.PM	_____
_____	4.PM	_____
_____	5.PM	_____
_____	6.PM	_____
_____	7.PM	_____
_____	8.PM	_____
_____	9.PM	_____
_____	10.PM	_____
_____	11.PM	_____
_____	12.AM	_____

BREAKFAST

LUNCH

DINNER

WATER

HAPPY SCALE

MY REWARD

DAILY PLANNER

TODAY IS /

WEATHER

TODAY I AM EXCITED ABOUT

TODAY I AM GRATEFUL FOR

TODAY'S TOP PRIORITY

1. _____
2. _____
3. _____

TO DO LIST

_____
_____
_____
_____
_____
_____
_____
_____
_____
_____
_____
_____
_____

TODAY'S SCHEDULE

PLAN		TRACK
_____	5.AM	_____
_____	6.AM	_____
_____	7.AM	_____
_____	8.AM	_____
_____	9.AM	_____
_____	10.AM	_____
_____	11.AM	_____
_____	12.PM	_____
_____	1.PM	_____
_____	3.PM	_____
_____	4.PM	_____
_____	5.PM	_____
_____	6.PM	_____
_____	7.PM	_____
_____	8.PM	_____
_____	9.PM	_____
_____	10.PM	_____
_____	11.PM	_____
_____	12.AM	

BREAKFAST

LUNCH

DINNER

WATER

HAPPY SCALE

MY REWARD

DAILY PLANNER

TODAY IS /

WEATHER

TODAY I AM EXCITED ABOUT

TODAY I AM GRATEFUL FOR

TODAY'S TOP PRIORITY

1. _____
2. _____
3. _____

TO DO LIST

_____
_____
_____
_____
_____
_____
_____
_____
_____
_____
_____
_____

TODAY'S SCHEDULE

PLAN		TRACK
_____	5.AM	_____
_____	6.AM	_____
_____	7.AM	_____
_____	8.AM	_____
_____	9.AM	_____
_____	10.AM	_____
_____	11.AM	_____
_____	12.PM	_____
_____	1.PM	_____
_____	3.PM	_____
_____	4.PM	_____
_____	5.PM	_____
_____	6.PM	_____
_____	7.PM	_____
_____	8.PM	_____
_____	9.PM	_____
_____	10.PM	_____
_____	11.PM	_____
_____	12.AM	_____

BREAKFAST

LUNCH

DINNER

WATER

HAPPY SCALE

MY REWARD

DAILY PLANNER

TODAY IS /

WEATHER

TODAY I AM EXCITED ABOUT

TODAY I AM GRATEFUL FOR

TODAY'S TOP PRIORITY

1. _____
2. _____
3. _____

TO DO LIST

TODAY'S SCHEDULE

PLAN		TRACK
_____	5.AM	_____
_____	6.AM	_____
_____	7.AM	_____
_____	8.AM	_____
_____	9.AM	_____
_____	10.AM	_____
_____	11.AM	_____
_____	12.PM	_____
_____	1.PM	_____
_____	3.PM	_____
_____	4.PM	_____
_____	5.PM	_____
_____	6.PM	_____
_____	7.PM	_____
_____	8.PM	_____
_____	9.PM	_____
_____	10.PM	_____
_____	11.PM	_____
_____	12.AM	_____

BREAKFAST

LUNCH

DINNER

WATER

HAPPY SCALE

MY REWARD

DAILY PLANNER

📅 TODAY IS /

WEATHER ☀️ ⛅ 🌧️ 🌬️ ❄️

TODAY I AM EXCITED ABOUT

TODAY I AM GRATEFUL FOR

TODAY'S TOP PRIORITY

1. _____
2. _____
3. _____

TO DO LIST

TODAY'S SCHEDULE

PLAN		TRACK
_____	5.AM	_____
_____	6.AM	_____
_____	7.AM	_____
_____	8.AM	_____
_____	9.AM	_____
_____	10.AM	_____
_____	11.AM	_____
_____	12.PM	_____
_____	1.PM	_____
_____	3.PM	_____
_____	4.PM	_____
_____	5.PM	_____
_____	6.PM	_____
_____	7.PM	_____
_____	8.PM	_____
_____	9.PM	_____
_____	10.PM	_____
_____	11.PM	_____
_____	12.AM	_____

BREAKFAST

LUNCH

DINNER

WATER

🥛 🥛 🥛 🥛 🥛
🥛 🥛 🥛 🥛 🥛

HAPPY SCALE

😀 🙂 😐 🙁 😫

MY REWARD

DAILY PLANNER

TODAY IS /   WEATHER ☀ ⛅ 🌧 💨 🌟

TODAY I AM EXCITED ABOUT

TODAY I AM GRATEFUL FOR

TODAY'S TOP PRIORITY

1. _____
2. _____
3. _____

TO DO LIST

_____
_____
_____
_____
_____
_____
_____
_____
_____
_____
_____

TODAY'S SCHEDULE

PLAN		TRACK
_____	5.AM	_____
_____	6.AM	_____
_____	7.AM	_____
_____	8.AM	_____
_____	9.AM	_____
_____	10.AM	_____
_____	11.AM	_____
_____	12.PM	_____
_____	1.PM	_____
_____	3.PM	_____
_____	4.PM	_____
_____	5.PM	_____
_____	6.PM	_____
_____	7.PM	_____
_____	8.PM	_____
_____	9.PM	_____
_____	10.PM	_____
_____	11.PM	_____
_____	12.AM	_____

BREAKFAST   LUNCH

DINNER   WATER

HAPPY SCALE

😀 🙂 😐 🙁 ☹

MY REWARD

DAILY PLANNER

TODAY IS /

WEATHER

TODAY I AM EXCITED ABOUT

TODAY I AM GRATEFUL FOR

TODAY'S TOP PRIORITY

1. _____
2. _____
3. _____

TO DO LIST

_____
_____
_____
_____
_____
_____
_____
_____
_____
_____

TODAY'S SCHEDULE

PLAN		TRACK
_____	5.AM	_____
_____	6.AM	_____
_____	7.AM	_____
_____	8.AM	_____
_____	9.AM	_____
_____	10.AM	_____
_____	11.AM	_____
_____	12.PM	_____
_____	1.PM	_____
_____	3.PM	_____
_____	4.PM	_____
_____	5.PM	_____
_____	6.PM	_____
_____	7.PM	_____
_____	8.PM	_____
_____	9.PM	_____
_____	10.PM	_____
_____	11.PM	_____
_____	12.AM	_____

BREAKFAST

LUNCH

DINNER

WATER

HAPPY SCALE

😀 🙂 😐 🙁 ☹️

MY REWARD

DAILY PLANNER

TODAY IS /

WEATHER

TODAY I AM EXCITED ABOUT

TODAY I AM GRATEFUL FOR

TODAY'S TOP PRIORITY

1. _____
2. _____
3. _____

TO DO LIST

_____
_____
_____
_____
_____
_____
_____
_____
_____
_____
_____
_____
_____

TODAY'S SCHEDULE

PLAN		TRACK
_____	5.AM	_____
_____	6.AM	_____
_____	7.AM	_____
_____	8.AM	_____
_____	9.AM	_____
_____	10.AM	_____
_____	11.AM	_____
_____	12.PM	_____
_____	1.PM	_____
_____	3.PM	_____
_____	4.PM	_____
_____	5.PM	_____
_____	6.PM	_____
_____	7.PM	_____
_____	8.PM	_____
_____	9.PM	_____
_____	10.PM	_____
_____	11.PM	_____
_____	12.AM	_____

BREAKFAST

LUNCH

DINNER

WATER

HAPPY SCALE

MY REWARD

DAILY PLANNER

TODAY IS /

WEATHER

TODAY I AM EXCITED ABOUT

TODAY I AM GRATEFUL FOR

TODAY'S TOP PRIORITY

1. _____
2. _____
3. _____

TO DO LIST

TODAY'S SCHEDULE

PLAN		TRACK
_____	5.AM	_____
_____	6.AM	_____
_____	7.AM	_____
_____	8.AM	_____
_____	9.AM	_____
_____	10.AM	_____
_____	11.AM	_____
_____	12.PM	_____
_____	1.PM	_____
_____	3.PM	_____
_____	4.PM	_____
_____	5.PM	_____
_____	6.PM	_____
_____	7.PM	_____
_____	8.PM	_____
_____	9.PM	_____
_____	10.PM	_____
_____	11.PM	_____
_____	12.AM	

BREAKFAST

LUNCH

DINNER

WATER

HAPPY SCALE

MY REWARD

DAILY PLANNER

TODAY IS /   WEATHER

TODAY I AM EXCITED ABOUT

TODAY I AM GRATEFUL FOR

TODAY'S TOP PRIORITY

1. _____
2. _____
3. _____

TO DO LIST

_____
_____
_____
_____
_____
_____
_____
_____
_____
_____

TODAY'S SCHEDULE

PLAN		TRACK
_____	5.AM	_____
_____	6.AM	_____
_____	7.AM	_____
_____	8.AM	_____
_____	9.AM	_____
_____	10.AM	_____
_____	11.AM	_____
_____	12.PM	_____
_____	1.PM	_____
_____	3.PM	_____
_____	4.PM	_____
_____	5.PM	_____
_____	6.PM	_____
_____	7.PM	_____
_____	8.PM	_____
_____	9.PM	_____
_____	10.PM	_____
_____	11.PM	_____
_____	12.AM	_____

BREAKFAST

LUNCH

DINNER

WATER

HAPPY SCALE

MY REWARD

DAILY PLANNER

TODAY IS /

WEATHER

TODAY I AM EXCITED ABOUT

TODAY I AM GRATEFUL FOR

TODAY'S TOP PRIORITY

1.

2.

3.

TO DO LIST

TODAY'S SCHEDULE

PLAN		TRACK
	5.AM	
	6.AM	
	7.AM	
	8.AM	
	9.AM	
	10.AM	
	11.AM	
	12.PM	
	1.PM	
	3.PM	
	4.PM	
	5.PM	
	6.PM	
	7.PM	
	8.PM	
	9.PM	
	10.PM	
	11.PM	
	12.AM	

BREAKFAST	LUNCH

DINNER	WATER

HAPPY SCALE

MY REWARD

DAILY PLANNER

TODAY IS /

WEATHER

TODAY I AM EXCITED ABOUT

TODAY I AM GRATEFUL FOR

TODAY'S TOP PRIORITY

1. _____

2. _____

3. _____

TO DO LIST

_____

_____

_____

_____

_____

_____

_____

_____

_____

_____

_____

TODAY'S SCHEDULE

PLAN		TRACK
_____	5.AM	_____
_____	6.AM	_____
_____	7.AM	_____
_____	8.AM	_____
_____	9.AM	_____
_____	10.AM	_____
_____	11.AM	_____
_____	12.PM	_____
_____	1.PM	_____
_____	3.PM	_____
_____	4.PM	_____
_____	5.PM	_____
_____	6.PM	_____
_____	7.PM	_____
_____	8.PM	_____
_____	9.PM	_____
_____	10.PM	_____
_____	11.PM	_____
_____	12.AM	_____

BREAKFAST

LUNCH

DINNER

WATER

HAPPY SCALE

MY REWARD

DAILY PLANNER

📅 TODAY IS /

WEATHER

TODAY I AM EXCITED ABOUT

TODAY I AM GRATEFUL FOR

TODAY'S TOP PRIORITY

1. _____
2. _____
3. _____

TO DO LIST

_____
_____
_____
_____
_____
_____
_____
_____
_____
_____
_____

TODAY'S SCHEDULE

PLAN		TRACK
_____	5.AM	_____
_____	6.AM	_____
_____	7.AM	_____
_____	8.AM	_____
_____	9.AM	_____
_____	10.AM	_____
_____	11.AM	_____
_____	12.PM	_____
_____	1.PM	_____
_____	3.PM	_____
_____	4.PM	_____
_____	5.PM	_____
_____	6.PM	_____
_____	7.PM	_____
_____	8.PM	_____
_____	9.PM	_____
_____	10.PM	_____
_____	11.PM	_____
_____	12.AM	_____

BREAKFAST

LUNCH

DINNER

WATER

HAPPY SCALE

😀 🙂 😐 ☹️ 😨

MY REWARD

DAILY PLANNER

📅 TODAY IS /   WEATHER ☀️ ⛅ 🌧️ 🌬️ 🌟

TODAY I AM EXCITED ABOUT

TODAY I AM GRATEFUL FOR

TODAY'S TOP PRIORITY

1. _____
2. _____
3. _____

TO DO LIST

_____
_____
_____
_____
_____
_____
_____
_____

TODAY'S SCHEDULE

PLAN		TRACK
_____	5.AM	_____
_____	6.AM	_____
_____	7.AM	_____
_____	8.AM	_____
_____	9.AM	_____
_____	10.AM	_____
_____	11.AM	_____
_____	12.PM	_____
_____	1.PM	_____
_____	3.PM	_____
_____	4.PM	_____
_____	5.PM	_____
_____	6.PM	_____
_____	7.PM	_____
_____	8.PM	_____
_____	9.PM	_____
_____	10.PM	_____
_____	11.PM	_____
_____	12.AM	_____

BREAKFAST

LUNCH

DINNER

WATER

🥛 🥛 🥛 🥛 🥛
🥛 🥛 🥛 🥛 🥛

HAPPY SCALE

😀 🙂 😐 🙁 😣

MY REWARD

DAILY PLANNER

TODAY IS /

WEATHER

TODAY I AM EXCITED ABOUT

TODAY I AM GRATEFUL FOR

TODAY'S TOP PRIORITY

1. _____
2. _____
3. _____

TO DO LIST

_____
_____
_____
_____
_____
_____
_____
_____
_____
_____
_____

TODAY'S SCHEDULE

PLAN		TRACK
_____	5.AM	_____
_____	6.AM	_____
_____	7.AM	_____
_____	8.AM	_____
_____	9.AM	_____
_____	10.AM	_____
_____	11.AM	_____
_____	12.PM	_____
_____	1.PM	_____
_____	3.PM	_____
_____	4.PM	_____
_____	5.PM	_____
_____	6.PM	_____
_____	7.PM	_____
_____	8.PM	_____
_____	9.PM	_____
_____	10.PM	_____
_____	11.PM	_____
_____	12.AM	_____

BREAKFAST

LUNCH

DINNER

WATER

HAPPY SCALE

MY REWARD

DAILY PLANNER

TODAY IS /

WEATHER

TODAY I AM EXCITED ABOUT

TODAY I AM GRATEFUL FOR

TODAY'S TOP PRIORITY

1. _____
2. _____
3. _____

TO DO LIST

_____
_____
_____
_____
_____
_____
_____
_____
_____
_____
_____

TODAY'S SCHEDULE

PLAN		TRACK
_____	5.AM	_____
_____	6.AM	_____
_____	7.AM	_____
_____	8.AM	_____
_____	9.AM	_____
_____	10.AM	_____
_____	11.AM	_____
_____	12.PM	_____
_____	1.PM	_____
_____	3.PM	_____
_____	4.PM	_____
_____	5.PM	_____
_____	6.PM	_____
_____	7.PM	_____
_____	8.PM	_____
_____	9.PM	_____
_____	10.PM	_____
_____	11.PM	_____
_____	12.AM	_____

BREAKFAST

LUNCH

DINNER

WATER

HAPPY SCALE

MY REWARD

DAILY PLANNER

TODAY IS /

WEATHER

TODAY I AM EXCITED ABOUT

TODAY I AM GRATEFUL FOR

TODAY'S TOP PRIORITY

1. _____
2. _____
3. _____

TO DO LIST

_____
_____
_____
_____
_____
_____
_____
_____
_____
_____
_____
_____

TODAY'S SCHEDULE

PLAN		TRACK
_____	5.AM	_____
_____	6.AM	_____
_____	7.AM	_____
_____	8.AM	_____
_____	9.AM	_____
_____	10.AM	_____
_____	11.AM	_____
_____	12.PM	_____
_____	1.PM	_____
_____	3.PM	_____
_____	4.PM	_____
_____	5.PM	_____
_____	6.PM	_____
_____	7.PM	_____
_____	8.PM	_____
_____	9.PM	_____
_____	10.PM	_____
_____	11.PM	_____
_____	12.AM	_____

BREAKFAST

LUNCH

DINNER

WATER

HAPPY SCALE

😀 🙂 😐 🙁 ☹️

MY REWARD

DAILY PLANNER

📅 TODAY IS /

WEATHER

TODAY I AM EXCITED ABOUT

TODAY I AM GRATEFUL FOR

TODAY'S TOP PRIORITY

1. _____
2. _____
3. _____

TO DO LIST

_____
_____
_____
_____
_____
_____
_____
_____
_____
_____
_____
_____

TODAY'S SCHEDULE

PLAN		TRACK
_____	5.AM	_____
_____	6.AM	_____
_____	7.AM	_____
_____	8.AM	_____
_____	9.AM	_____
_____	10.AM	_____
_____	11.AM	_____
_____	12.PM	_____
_____	1.PM	_____
_____	3.PM	_____
_____	4.PM	_____
_____	5.PM	_____
_____	6.PM	_____
_____	7.PM	_____
_____	8.PM	_____
_____	9.PM	_____
_____	10.PM	_____
_____	11.PM	_____
_____	12.AM	_____

BREAKFAST

LUNCH

DINNER

WATER

HAPPY SCALE

MY REWARD

DAILY PLANNER

TODAY IS /

WEATHER

TODAY I AM EXCITED ABOUT

TODAY I AM GRATEFUL FOR

TODAY'S TOP PRIORITY

1.
2.
3.

TO DO LIST

TODAY'S SCHEDULE

PLAN		TRACK
	5.AM	
	6.AM	
	7.AM	
	8.AM	
	9.AM	
	10.AM	
	11.AM	
	12.PM	
	1.PM	
	3.PM	
	4.PM	
	5.PM	
	6.PM	
	7.PM	
	8.PM	
	9.PM	
	10.PM	
	11.PM	
	12.AM	

BREAKFAST

LUNCH

DINNER

WATER

HAPPY SCALE

MY REWARD

DAILY PLANNER

TODAY IS /

WEATHER

TODAY I AM EXCITED ABOUT

TODAY I AM GRATEFUL FOR

TODAY'S TOP PRIORITY

1. _____
2. _____
3. _____

TO DO LIST

_____
_____
_____
_____
_____
_____
_____
_____
_____
_____
_____

TODAY'S SCHEDULE

PLAN		TRACK
_____	5.AM	_____
_____	6.AM	_____
_____	7.AM	_____
_____	8.AM	_____
_____	9.AM	_____
_____	10.AM	_____
_____	11.AM	_____
_____	12.PM	_____
_____	1.PM	_____
_____	3.PM	_____
_____	4.PM	_____
_____	5.PM	_____
_____	6.PM	_____
_____	7.PM	_____
_____	8.PM	_____
_____	9.PM	_____
_____	10.PM	_____
_____	11.PM	_____
_____	12.AM	_____

BREAKFAST

LUNCH

DINNER

WATER

HAPPY SCALE

MY REWARD

DAILY PLANNER

TODAY IS /

WEATHER

TODAY I AM EXCITED ABOUT

TODAY I AM GRATEFUL FOR

TODAY'S TOP PRIORITY

1. _____

2. _____

3. _____

TO DO LIST

_____

_____

_____

_____

_____

_____

_____

_____

_____

_____

_____

TODAY'S SCHEDULE

PLAN		TRACK
_____	5.AM	_____
_____	6.AM	_____
_____	7.AM	_____
_____	8.AM	_____
_____	9.AM	_____
_____	10.AM	_____
_____	11.AM	_____
_____	12.PM	_____
_____	1.PM	_____
_____	3.PM	_____
_____	4.PM	_____
_____	5.PM	_____
_____	6.PM	_____
_____	7.PM	_____
_____	8.PM	_____
_____	9.PM	_____
_____	10.PM	_____
_____	11.PM	_____
_____	12.AM	_____

BREAKFAST

LUNCH

DINNER

WATER

HAPPY SCALE

MY REWARD

DAILY PLANNER

📅 TODAY IS /

WEATHER ☀ ⛅ 🌧 🌬 ❄

TODAY I AM EXCITED ABOUT

TODAY I AM GRATEFUL FOR

TODAY'S TOP PRIORITY

1. _____
2. _____
3. _____

TO DO LIST

_____
_____
_____
_____
_____
_____
_____
_____
_____

TODAY'S SCHEDULE

PLAN		TRACK
_____	5.AM	_____
_____	6.AM	_____
_____	7.AM	_____
_____	8.AM	_____
_____	9.AM	_____
_____	10.AM	_____
_____	11.AM	_____
_____	12.PM	_____
_____	1.PM	_____
_____	3.PM	_____
_____	4.PM	_____
_____	5.PM	_____
_____	6.PM	_____
_____	7.PM	_____
_____	8.PM	_____
_____	9.PM	_____
_____	10.PM	_____
_____	11.PM	_____
_____	12.AM	_____

BREAKFAST

LUNCH

DINNER

WATER

HAPPY SCALE

MY REWARD

DAILY PLANNER

TODAY IS /　　　　　　　　　　WEATHER

TODAY I AM EXCITED ABOUT	TODAY I AM GRATEFUL FOR

TODAY'S TOP PRIORITY

1. _____
2. _____
3. _____

TODAY'S SCHEDULE

PLAN		TRACK
_____	5.AM	_____
_____	6.AM	_____
_____	7.AM	_____
_____	8.AM	_____
_____	9.AM	_____
_____	10.AM	_____
_____	11.AM	_____
_____	12.PM	_____
_____	1.PM	_____
_____	3.PM	_____
_____	4.PM	_____
_____	5.PM	_____
_____	6.PM	_____
_____	7.PM	_____
_____	8.PM	_____
_____	9.PM	_____
_____	10.PM	_____
_____	11.PM	_____
_____	12.AM	_____

TO DO LIST

_____
_____
_____
_____
_____
_____
_____
_____
_____
_____
_____

BREAKFAST	LUNCH

DINNER	WATER

HAPPY SCALE

MY REWARD

DAILY PLANNER

TODAY IS /   WEATHER

TODAY I AM EXCITED ABOUT

TODAY I AM GRATEFUL FOR

TODAY'S TOP PRIORITY

1. _____
2. _____
3. _____

TO DO LIST

_____
_____
_____
_____
_____
_____
_____
_____
_____
_____
_____

TODAY'S SCHEDULE

PLAN		TRACK
_____	5.AM	_____
_____	6.AM	_____
_____	7.AM	_____
_____	8.AM	_____
_____	9.AM	_____
_____	10.AM	_____
_____	11.AM	_____
_____	12.PM	_____
_____	1.PM	_____
_____	3.PM	_____
_____	4.PM	_____
_____	5.PM	_____
_____	6.PM	_____
_____	7.PM	_____
_____	8.PM	_____
_____	9.PM	_____
_____	10.PM	_____
_____	11.PM	_____
_____	12.AM	_____

BREAKFAST   LUNCH

DINNER   WATER

HAPPY SCALE

MY REWARD

DAILY PLANNER

TODAY IS /

WEATHER

TODAY I AM EXCITED ABOUT

TODAY I AM GRATEFUL FOR

TODAY'S TOP PRIORITY

1. _____
2. _____
3. _____

TO DO LIST

TODAY'S SCHEDULE

PLAN		TRACK
_____	5.AM	_____
_____	6.AM	_____
_____	7.AM	_____
_____	8.AM	_____
_____	9.AM	_____
_____	10.AM	_____
_____	11.AM	_____
_____	12.PM	_____
_____	1.PM	_____
_____	3.PM	_____
_____	4.PM	_____
_____	5.PM	_____
_____	6.PM	_____
_____	7.PM	_____
_____	8.PM	_____
_____	9.PM	_____
_____	10.PM	_____
_____	11.PM	_____
_____	12.AM	_____

BREAKFAST

LUNCH

DINNER

WATER

HAPPY SCALE

MY REWARD

DAILY PLANNER

📅 TODAY IS /

WEATHER

TODAY I AM EXCITED ABOUT

TODAY I AM GRATEFUL FOR

TODAY'S TOP PRIORITY

1. _____
2. _____
3. _____

TO DO LIST

_____
_____
_____
_____
_____
_____
_____
_____
_____
_____
_____
_____

TODAY'S SCHEDULE

PLAN		TRACK
	5.AM	
	6.AM	
	7.AM	
	8.AM	
	9.AM	
	10.AM	
	11.AM	
	12.PM	
	1.PM	
	3.PM	
	4.PM	
	5.PM	
	6.PM	
	7.PM	
	8.PM	
	9.PM	
	10.PM	
	11.PM	
	12.AM	

BREAKFAST

LUNCH

DINNER

WATER

HAPPY SCALE

MY REWARD

DAILY PLANNER

TODAY IS /

WEATHER

TODAY I AM EXCITED ABOUT

TODAY I AM GRATEFUL FOR

TODAY'S TOP PRIORITY

1. _____
2. _____
3. _____

TO DO LIST

_____
_____
_____
_____
_____
_____
_____
_____
_____
_____
_____

TODAY'S SCHEDULE

PLAN		TRACK
_____	5.AM	_____
_____	6.AM	_____
_____	7.AM	_____
_____	8.AM	_____
_____	9.AM	_____
_____	10.AM	_____
_____	11.AM	_____
_____	12.PM	_____
_____	1.PM	_____
_____	3.PM	_____
_____	4.PM	_____
_____	5.PM	_____
_____	6.PM	_____
_____	7.PM	_____
_____	8.PM	_____
_____	9.PM	_____
_____	10.PM	_____
_____	11.PM	_____
_____	12.AM	_____

BREAKFAST

LUNCH

DINNER

WATER

HAPPY SCALE

MY REWARD

DAILY PLANNER

TODAY IS /

WEATHER

TODAY I AM EXCITED ABOUT

TODAY I AM GRATEFUL FOR

TODAY'S TOP PRIORITY

1. _____
2. _____
3. _____

TO DO LIST

_____
_____
_____
_____
_____
_____
_____
_____
_____
_____
_____
_____

TODAY'S SCHEDULE

PLAN		TRACK
_____	5.AM	_____
_____	6.AM	_____
_____	7.AM	_____
_____	8.AM	_____
_____	9.AM	_____
_____	10.AM	_____
_____	11.AM	_____
_____	12.PM	_____
_____	1.PM	_____
_____	3.PM	_____
_____	4.PM	_____
_____	5.PM	_____
_____	6.PM	_____
_____	7.PM	_____
_____	8.PM	_____
_____	9.PM	_____
_____	10.PM	_____
_____	11.PM	_____
_____	12.AM	_____

BREAKFAST

LUNCH

DINNER

WATER

HAPPY SCALE

MY REWARD

DAILY PLANNER

TODAY IS /

WEATHER

TODAY I AM EXCITED ABOUT

TODAY I AM GRATEFUL FOR

TODAY'S TOP PRIORITY

1. _____
2. _____
3. _____

TO DO LIST

_____
_____
_____
_____
_____
_____
_____
_____
_____
_____
_____
_____

TODAY'S SCHEDULE

PLAN		TRACK
_____	5.AM	_____
_____	6.AM	_____
_____	7.AM	_____
_____	8.AM	_____
_____	9.AM	_____
_____	10.AM	_____
_____	11.AM	_____
_____	12.PM	_____
_____	1.PM	_____
_____	3.PM	_____
_____	4.PM	_____
_____	5.PM	_____
_____	6.PM	_____
_____	7.PM	_____
_____	8.PM	_____
_____	9.PM	_____
_____	10.PM	_____
_____	11.PM	_____
_____	12.AM	_____

BREAKFAST

LUNCH

DINNER

WATER

HAPPY SCALE

MY REWARD

DAILY PLANNER

TODAY IS /

WEATHER

TODAY I AM EXCITED ABOUT

TODAY I AM GRATEFUL FOR

TODAY'S TOP PRIORITY

1. _____
2. _____
3. _____

TO DO LIST

_____
_____
_____
_____
_____
_____
_____
_____
_____
_____
_____

TODAY'S SCHEDULE

PLAN		TRACK
_____	5.AM	_____
_____	6.AM	_____
_____	7.AM	_____
_____	8.AM	_____
_____	9.AM	_____
_____	10.AM	_____
_____	11.AM	_____
_____	12.PM	_____
_____	1.PM	_____
_____	3.PM	_____
_____	4.PM	_____
_____	5.PM	_____
_____	6.PM	_____
_____	7.PM	_____
_____	8.PM	_____
_____	9.PM	_____
_____	10.PM	_____
_____	11.PM	_____
_____	12.AM	_____

BREAKFAST

LUNCH

DINNER

WATER

HAPPY SCALE

MY REWARD

DAILY PLANNER

TODAY IS /

WEATHER

TODAY I AM EXCITED ABOUT

TODAY I AM GRATEFUL FOR

TODAY'S TOP PRIORITY

1. _____
2. _____
3. _____

TO DO LIST

TODAY'S SCHEDULE

PLAN		TRACK
	5.AM	
	6.AM	
	7.AM	
	8.AM	
	9.AM	
	10.AM	
	11.AM	
	12.PM	
	1.PM	
	3.PM	
	4.PM	
	5.PM	
	6.PM	
	7.PM	
	8.PM	
	9.PM	
	10.PM	
	11.PM	
	12.AM	

BREAKFAST

LUNCH

DINNER

WATER

HAPPY SCALE

MY REWARD

DAILY PLANNER

TODAY IS /   WEATHER ☀ ⛅ 🌧 🌬 ☀

TODAY I AM EXCITED ABOUT

TODAY I AM GRATEFUL FOR

TODAY'S TOP PRIORITY

1. _____

2. _____

3. _____

TO DO LIST

_____

_____

_____

_____

_____

_____

_____

_____

_____

_____

_____

TODAY'S SCHEDULE

PLAN		TRACK
_____	5.AM	_____
_____	6.AM	_____
_____	7.AM	_____
_____	8.AM	_____
_____	9.AM	_____
_____	10.AM	_____
_____	11.AM	_____
_____	12.PM	_____
_____	1.PM	_____
_____	3.PM	_____
_____	4.PM	_____
_____	5.PM	_____
_____	6.PM	_____
_____	7.PM	_____
_____	8.PM	_____
_____	9.PM	_____
_____	10.PM	_____
_____	11.PM	_____
_____	12.AM	_____

BREAKFAST   LUNCH

DINNER   WATER

🥛 🥛 🥛 🥛 🥛
🥛 🥛 🥛 🥛 🥛

HAPPY SCALE

😀 🙂 😐 🙁 😫

MY REWARD

DAILY PLANNER

TODAY IS /

WEATHER

TODAY I AM EXCITED ABOUT

TODAY I AM GRATEFUL FOR

TODAY'S TOP PRIORITY

1. _____
2. _____
3. _____

TO DO LIST

_____
_____
_____
_____
_____
_____
_____
_____
_____
_____
_____
_____

TODAY'S SCHEDULE

PLAN		TRACK
_____	5.AM	_____
_____	6.AM	_____
_____	7.AM	_____
_____	8.AM	_____
_____	9.AM	_____
_____	10.AM	_____
_____	11.AM	_____
_____	12.PM	_____
_____	1.PM	_____
_____	3.PM	_____
_____	4.PM	_____
_____	5.PM	_____
_____	6.PM	_____
_____	7.PM	_____
_____	8.PM	_____
_____	9.PM	_____
_____	10.PM	_____
_____	11.PM	_____
_____	12.AM	_____

BREAKFAST

LUNCH

DINNER

WATER

HAPPY SCALE

MY REWARD

DAILY PLANNER

TODAY IS /

WEATHER

TODAY I AM EXCITED ABOUT

TODAY I AM GRATEFUL FOR

TODAY'S TOP PRIORITY

1. _____
2. _____
3. _____

TO DO LIST

_____
_____
_____
_____
_____
_____
_____
_____
_____

TODAY'S SCHEDULE

PLAN		TRACK
_____	5.AM	_____
_____	6.AM	_____
_____	7.AM	_____
_____	8.AM	_____
_____	9.AM	_____
_____	10.AM	_____
_____	11.AM	_____
_____	12.PM	_____
_____	1.PM	_____
_____	3.PM	_____
_____	4.PM	_____
_____	5.PM	_____
_____	6.PM	_____
_____	7.PM	_____
_____	8.PM	_____
_____	9.PM	_____
_____	10.PM	_____
_____	11.PM	_____
_____	12.AM	_____

BREAKFAST

LUNCH

DINNER

WATER

HAPPY SCALE

😀 🙂 😐 🙁 😫

MY REWARD

DAILY PLANNER

TODAY IS /

WEATHER

TODAY I AM EXCITED ABOUT

TODAY I AM GRATEFUL FOR

TODAY'S TOP PRIORITY

1. _____
2. _____
3. _____

TO DO LIST

_____
_____
_____
_____
_____
_____
_____
_____
_____
_____
_____
_____

TODAY'S SCHEDULE

PLAN		TRACK
_____	5.AM	_____
_____	6.AM	_____
_____	7.AM	_____
_____	8.AM	_____
_____	9.AM	_____
_____	10.AM	_____
_____	11.AM	_____
_____	12.PM	_____
_____	1.PM	_____
_____	3.PM	_____
_____	4.PM	_____
_____	5.PM	_____
_____	6.PM	_____
_____	7.PM	_____
_____	8.PM	_____
_____	9.PM	_____
_____	10.PM	_____
_____	11.PM	_____
_____	12.AM	_____

BREAKFAST

LUNCH

DINNER

WATER

HAPPY SCALE

MY REWARD

DAILY PLANNER

📅 TODAY IS /

WEATHER

TODAY I AM EXCITED ABOUT

TODAY I AM GRATEFUL FOR

TODAY'S TOP PRIORITY

1. _____
2. _____
3. _____

TO DO LIST

_____
_____
_____
_____
_____
_____
_____
_____
_____
_____
_____

TODAY'S SCHEDULE

PLAN		TRACK
_____	5.AM	_____
_____	6.AM	_____
_____	7.AM	_____
_____	8.AM	_____
_____	9.AM	_____
_____	10.AM	_____
_____	11.AM	_____
_____	12.PM	_____
_____	1.PM	_____
_____	3.PM	_____
_____	4.PM	_____
_____	5.PM	_____
_____	6.PM	_____
_____	7.PM	_____
_____	8.PM	_____
_____	9.PM	_____
_____	10.PM	_____
_____	11.PM	_____
_____	12.AM	_____

BREAKFAST

LUNCH

DINNER

WATER

HAPPY SCALE

😃 🙂 😐 ☹️ 😫

MY REWARD

DAILY PLANNER

TODAY IS /

WEATHER

TODAY I AM EXCITED ABOUT

TODAY I AM GRATEFUL FOR

TODAY'S TOP PRIORITY

1. _____
2. _____
3. _____

TO DO LIST

_____
_____
_____
_____
_____
_____
_____
_____
_____
_____
_____

TODAY'S SCHEDULE

PLAN		TRACK
_____	5.AM	_____
_____	6.AM	_____
_____	7.AM	_____
_____	8.AM	_____
_____	9.AM	_____
_____	10.AM	_____
_____	11.AM	_____
_____	12.PM	_____
_____	1.PM	_____
_____	3.PM	_____
_____	4.PM	_____
_____	5.PM	_____
_____	6.PM	_____
_____	7.PM	_____
_____	8.PM	_____
_____	9.PM	_____
_____	10.PM	_____
_____	11.PM	_____
_____	12.AM	_____

BREAKFAST

LUNCH

DINNER

WATER

HAPPY SCALE

MY REWARD

DAILY PLANNER

TODAY IS /

WEATHER

TODAY I AM EXCITED ABOUT

TODAY I AM GRATEFUL FOR

TODAY'S TOP PRIORITY

1. _____
2. _____
3. _____

TO DO LIST

_____
_____
_____
_____
_____
_____
_____
_____
_____
_____
_____
_____
_____

TODAY'S SCHEDULE

PLAN		TRACK
_____	5.AM	_____
_____	6.AM	_____
_____	7.AM	_____
_____	8.AM	_____
_____	9.AM	_____
_____	10.AM	_____
_____	11.AM	_____
_____	12.PM	_____
_____	1.PM	_____
_____	3.PM	_____
_____	4.PM	_____
_____	5.PM	_____
_____	6.PM	_____
_____	7.PM	_____
_____	8.PM	_____
_____	9.PM	_____
_____	10.PM	_____
_____	11.PM	_____
_____	12.AM	_____

BREAKFAST

LUNCH

DINNER

WATER

HAPPY SCALE

MY REWARD

DAILY PLANNER

📅 TODAY IS /

WEATHER ☀️ ⛅ 🌧️ 🌬️ 🌫️

TODAY I AM EXCITED ABOUT

TODAY I AM GRATEFUL FOR

TODAY'S TOP PRIORITY

1. _____
2. _____
3. _____

TO DO LIST

_____
_____
_____
_____
_____
_____
_____
_____
_____
_____
_____
_____

TODAY'S SCHEDULE

PLAN		TRACK
_____	5.AM	_____
_____	6.AM	_____
_____	7.AM	_____
_____	8.AM	_____
_____	9.AM	_____
_____	10.AM	_____
_____	11.AM	_____
_____	12.PM	_____
_____	1.PM	_____
_____	3.PM	_____
_____	4.PM	_____
_____	5.PM	_____
_____	6.PM	_____
_____	7.PM	_____
_____	8.PM	_____
_____	9.PM	_____
_____	10.PM	_____
_____	11.PM	_____
_____	12.AM	_____

BREAKFAST

LUNCH

DINNER

WATER

🥤 🥤 🥤 🥤 🥤
🥤 🥤 🥤 🥤 🥤

HAPPY SCALE

😃 🙂 😐 🙁 😫

MY REWARD

DAILY PLANNER

TODAY IS /

WEATHER

TODAY I AM EXCITED ABOUT

TODAY I AM GRATEFUL FOR

TODAY'S TOP PRIORITY

1. _____
2. _____
3. _____

TO DO LIST

_____
_____
_____
_____
_____
_____
_____
_____
_____
_____
_____

TODAY'S SCHEDULE

PLAN		TRACK
_____	5.AM	_____
_____	6.AM	_____
_____	7.AM	_____
_____	8.AM	_____
_____	9.AM	_____
_____	10.AM	_____
_____	11.AM	_____
_____	12.PM	_____
_____	1.PM	_____
_____	3.PM	_____
_____	4.PM	_____
_____	5.PM	_____
_____	6.PM	_____
_____	7.PM	_____
_____	8.PM	_____
_____	9.PM	_____
_____	10.PM	_____
_____	11.PM	_____
_____	12.AM	_____

BREAKFAST

LUNCH

DINNER

WATER

HAPPY SCALE

MY REWARD

DAILY PLANNER

TODAY IS /   WEATHER

TODAY I AM EXCITED ABOUT

TODAY I AM GRATEFUL FOR

TODAY'S TOP PRIORITY

1.
2.
3.

TO DO LIST

TODAY'S SCHEDULE

PLAN		TRACK
	5.AM	
	6.AM	
	7.AM	
	8.AM	
	9.AM	
	10.AM	
	11.AM	
	12.PM	
	1.PM	
	3.PM	
	4.PM	
	5.PM	
	6.PM	
	7.PM	
	8.PM	
	9.PM	
	10.PM	
	11.PM	
	12.AM	

BREAKFAST

LUNCH

DINNER

WATER

HAPPY SCALE

MY REWARD

DAILY PLANNER

📅 TODAY IS /

WEATHER ☀ ⛅ 🌧 💨 🌟

TODAY I AM EXCITED ABOUT

TODAY I AM GRATEFUL FOR

TODAY'S TOP PRIORITY

1. _____
2. _____
3. _____

TO DO LIST

_____
_____
_____
_____
_____
_____
_____
_____
_____
_____

TODAY'S SCHEDULE

PLAN		TRACK
_____	5.AM	_____
_____	6.AM	_____
_____	7.AM	_____
_____	8.AM	_____
_____	9.AM	_____
_____	10.AM	_____
_____	11.AM	_____
_____	12.PM	_____
_____	1.PM	_____
_____	3.PM	_____
_____	4.PM	_____
_____	5.PM	_____
_____	6.PM	_____
_____	7.PM	_____
_____	8.PM	_____
_____	9.PM	_____
_____	10.PM	_____
_____	11.PM	_____
_____	12.AM	_____

BREAKFAST

LUNCH

DINNER

WATER

HAPPY SCALE

😀 🙂 😐 🙁 ☹️

MY REWARD

DAILY PLANNER

📅 TODAY IS /

WEATHER ☀️ ⛅ 🌧️ 🌬️ ❄️

TODAY I AM EXCITED ABOUT

TODAY I AM GRATEFUL FOR

TODAY'S TOP PRIORITY

1. _____
2. _____
3. _____

TO DO LIST

_____
_____
_____
_____
_____
_____
_____
_____
_____
_____
_____

TODAY'S SCHEDULE

PLAN		TRACK
_____	5.AM	_____
_____	6.AM	_____
_____	7.AM	_____
_____	8.AM	_____
_____	9.AM	_____
_____	10.AM	_____
_____	11.AM	_____
_____	12.PM	_____
_____	1.PM	_____
_____	3.PM	_____
_____	4.PM	_____
_____	5.PM	_____
_____	6.PM	_____
_____	7.PM	_____
_____	8.PM	_____
_____	9.PM	_____
_____	10.PM	_____
_____	11.PM	_____
_____	12.AM	

BREAKFAST

LUNCH

DINNER

WATER

🥛 🥛 🥛 🥛 🥛
🥛 🥛 🥛 🥛 🥛

HAPPY SCALE

😃 🙂 😐 🙁 ☹️

MY REWARD

DAILY PLANNER

TODAY IS /

WEATHER

TODAY I AM EXCITED ABOUT

TODAY I AM GRATEFUL FOR

TODAY'S TOP PRIORITY

1. _____
2. _____
3. _____

TO DO LIST

_____
_____
_____
_____
_____
_____
_____
_____
_____
_____
_____
_____

TODAY'S SCHEDULE

PLAN		TRACK
_____	5.AM	_____
_____	6.AM	_____
_____	7.AM	_____
_____	8.AM	_____
_____	9.AM	_____
_____	10.AM	_____
_____	11.AM	_____
_____	12.PM	_____
_____	1.PM	_____
_____	3.PM	_____
_____	4.PM	_____
_____	5.PM	_____
_____	6.PM	_____
_____	7.PM	_____
_____	8.PM	_____
_____	9.PM	_____
_____	10.PM	_____
_____	11.PM	_____
_____	12.AM	_____

BREAKFAST

LUNCH

DINNER

WATER

HAPPY SCALE

MY REWARD

DAILY PLANNER

TODAY IS /

WEATHER

TODAY I AM EXCITED ABOUT

TODAY I AM GRATEFUL FOR

TODAY'S TOP PRIORITY

1. _____
2. _____
3. _____

TO DO LIST

_____
_____
_____
_____
_____
_____
_____
_____
_____
_____
_____

TODAY'S SCHEDULE

PLAN		TRACK
_____	5.AM	_____
_____	6.AM	_____
_____	7.AM	_____
_____	8.AM	_____
_____	9.AM	_____
_____	10.AM	_____
_____	11.AM	_____
_____	12.PM	_____
_____	1.PM	_____
_____	3.PM	_____
_____	4.PM	_____
_____	5.PM	_____
_____	6.PM	_____
_____	7.PM	_____
_____	8.PM	_____
_____	9.PM	_____
_____	10.PM	_____
_____	11.PM	_____
_____	12.AM	

BREAKFAST

LUNCH

DINNER

WATER

HAPPY SCALE

MY REWARD

DAILY PLANNER

📅 TODAY IS /

WEATHER ☀️ ⛅ 🌧️ 🌬️ ☀️

TODAY I AM EXCITED ABOUT

TODAY I AM GRATEFUL FOR

TODAY'S TOP PRIORITY

1. _____
2. _____
3. _____

TO DO LIST

_____
_____
_____
_____
_____
_____
_____
_____
_____
_____
_____
_____

TODAY'S SCHEDULE

PLAN		TRACK
_____	5.AM	_____
_____	6.AM	_____
_____	7.AM	_____
_____	8.AM	_____
_____	9.AM	_____
_____	10.AM	_____
_____	11.AM	_____
_____	12.PM	_____
_____	1.PM	_____
_____	3.PM	_____
_____	4.PM	_____
_____	5.PM	_____
_____	6.PM	_____
_____	7.PM	_____
_____	8.PM	_____
_____	9.PM	_____
_____	10.PM	_____
_____	11.PM	_____
_____	12.AM	_____

BREAKFAST

LUNCH

DINNER

WATER

HAPPY SCALE

😀 🙂 😐 🙁 ☹️

MY REWARD

DAILY PLANNER

TODAY IS /   WEATHER

TODAY I AM EXCITED ABOUT

TODAY I AM GRATEFUL FOR

TODAY'S TOP PRIORITY

1. _____
2. _____
3. _____

TO DO LIST

TODAY'S SCHEDULE

PLAN		TRACK
_____	5.AM	_____
_____	6.AM	_____
_____	7.AM	_____
_____	8.AM	_____
_____	9.AM	_____
_____	10.AM	_____
_____	11.AM	_____
_____	12.PM	_____
_____	1.PM	_____
_____	3.PM	_____
_____	4.PM	_____
_____	5.PM	_____
_____	6.PM	_____
_____	7.PM	_____
_____	8.PM	_____
_____	9.PM	_____
_____	10.PM	_____
_____	11.PM	_____
_____	12.AM	_____

BREAKFAST   LUNCH

DINNER   WATER

HAPPY SCALE

MY REWARD

DAILY PLANNER

TODAY IS /

WEATHER

TODAY I AM EXCITED ABOUT

TODAY I AM GRATEFUL FOR

TODAY'S TOP PRIORITY

1. _____

2. _____

3. _____

TO DO LIST

_____
_____
_____
_____
_____
_____
_____
_____
_____
_____
_____
_____

TODAY'S SCHEDULE

PLAN		TRACK
_____	5.AM	
_____	6.AM	
_____	7.AM	
_____	8.AM	_____
_____	9.AM	_____
_____	10.AM	_____
_____	11.AM	_____
_____	12.PM	_____
_____	1.PM	_____
_____	3.PM	_____
_____	4.PM	_____
_____	5.PM	_____
_____	6.PM	_____
_____	7.PM	_____
_____	8.PM	_____
_____	9.PM	_____
_____	10.PM	_____
_____	11.PM	_____
_____	12.AM	_____

BREAKFAST

LUNCH

DINNER

WATER

HAPPY SCALE

MY REWARD

DAILY PLANNER

📅 TODAY IS /

WEATHER

TODAY I AM EXCITED ABOUT

TODAY I AM GRATEFUL FOR

TODAY'S TOP PRIORITY

1. _____
2. _____
3. _____

TO DO LIST

_____
_____
_____
_____
_____
_____
_____
_____
_____
_____
_____
_____

TODAY'S SCHEDULE

PLAN		TRACK
_____	5.AM	_____
_____	6.AM	_____
_____	7.AM	_____
_____	8.AM	_____
_____	9.AM	_____
_____	10.AM	_____
_____	11.AM	_____
_____	12.PM	_____
_____	1.PM	_____
_____	3.PM	_____
_____	4.PM	_____
_____	5.PM	_____
_____	6.PM	_____
_____	7.PM	_____
_____	8.PM	_____
_____	9.PM	_____
_____	10.PM	_____
_____	11.PM	_____
_____	12.AM	_____

BREAKFAST

LUNCH

DINNER

WATER

HAPPY SCALE

😃 🙂 😐 🙁 ☹️

MY REWARD

DAILY PLANNER

📅 TODAY IS /

WEATHER ☀️ ⛅ 🌧️ 🌬️ 🌀

TODAY I AM EXCITED ABOUT

TODAY I AM GRATEFUL FOR

TODAY'S TOP PRIORITY

1. _____
2. _____
3. _____

TO DO LIST

_____
_____
_____
_____
_____
_____
_____
_____
_____
_____
_____

TODAY'S SCHEDULE

PLAN		TRACK
_____	5.AM	_____
_____	6.AM	_____
_____	7.AM	_____
_____	8.AM	_____
_____	9.AM	_____
_____	10.AM	_____
_____	11.AM	_____
_____	12.PM	_____
_____	1.PM	_____
_____	3.PM	_____
_____	4.PM	_____
_____	5.PM	_____
_____	6.PM	_____
_____	7.PM	_____
_____	8.PM	_____
_____	9.PM	_____
_____	10.PM	_____
_____	11.PM	_____
_____	12.AM	

BREAKFAST

LUNCH

DINNER

WATER
🥛 🥛 🥛 🥛 🥛
🥛 🥛 🥛 🥛 🥛

HAPPY SCALE

😀 🙂 😐 🙁 😫

MY REWARD

DAILY PLANNER

📅 TODAY IS /

WEATHER

TODAY I AM EXCITED ABOUT

TODAY I AM GRATEFUL FOR

TODAY'S TOP PRIORITY

1.
2.
3.

TO DO LIST

TODAY'S SCHEDULE

PLAN		TRACK
	5.AM	
	6.AM	
	7.AM	
	8.AM	
	9.AM	
	10.AM	
	11.AM	
	12.PM	
	1.PM	
	3.PM	
	4.PM	
	5.PM	
	6.PM	
	7.PM	
	8.PM	
	9.PM	
	10.PM	
	11.PM	
	12.AM	

BREAKFAST

LUNCH

DINNER

WATER

HAPPY SCALE

😀 🙂 😐 🙁 ☹️

MY REWARD

DAILY PLANNER

📅 TODAY IS /

WEATHER

TODAY I AM EXCITED ABOUT

TODAY I AM GRATEFUL FOR

TODAY'S TOP PRIORITY

1. _____
2. _____
3. _____

TO DO LIST

_____
_____
_____
_____
_____
_____
_____
_____
_____
_____
_____
_____

TODAY'S SCHEDULE

PLAN		TRACK
_____	5.AM	_____
_____	6.AM	_____
_____	7.AM	_____
_____	8.AM	_____
_____	9.AM	_____
_____	10.AM	_____
_____	11.AM	_____
_____	12.PM	_____
_____	1.PM	_____
_____	3.PM	_____
_____	4.PM	_____
_____	5.PM	_____
_____	6.PM	_____
_____	7.PM	_____
_____	8.PM	_____
_____	9.PM	_____
_____	10.PM	_____
_____	11.PM	_____
_____	12.AM	_____

BREAKFAST

LUNCH

DINNER

WATER

HAPPY SCALE

😃 🙂 😐 🙁 ☹️

MY REWARD

DAILY PLANNER

TODAY IS /

WEATHER

TODAY I AM EXCITED ABOUT

TODAY I AM GRATEFUL FOR

TODAY'S TOP PRIORITY

1. _____
2. _____
3. _____

TO DO LIST

_____
_____
_____
_____
_____
_____
_____
_____
_____
_____
_____

TODAY'S SCHEDULE

PLAN		TRACK
_____	5.AM	_____
_____	6.AM	_____
_____	7.AM	_____
_____	8.AM	_____
_____	9.AM	_____
_____	10.AM	_____
_____	11.AM	_____
_____	12.PM	_____
_____	1.PM	_____
_____	3.PM	_____
_____	4.PM	_____
_____	5.PM	_____
_____	6.PM	_____
_____	7.PM	_____
_____	8.PM	_____
_____	9.PM	_____
_____	10.PM	_____
_____	11.PM	_____
_____	12.AM	_____

BREAKFAST

LUNCH

DINNER

WATER

HAPPY SCALE

MY REWARD

DAILY PLANNER

▦ TODAY IS /   WEATHER ☼ ⛅ 🌧 🌬 ☀

TODAY I AM EXCITED ABOUT

[ ]

TODAY I AM GRATEFUL FOR

[ ]

TODAY'S TOP PRIORITY

1. _____
2. _____
3. _____

TO DO LIST

_____
_____
_____
_____
_____
_____
_____
_____
_____
_____

TODAY'S SCHEDULE

PLAN		TRACK
_____	5.AM	_____
_____	6.AM	_____
_____	7.AM	_____
_____	8.AM	_____
_____	9.AM	_____
_____	10.AM	_____
_____	11.AM	_____
_____	12.PM	_____
_____	1.PM	_____
_____	3.PM	_____
_____	4.PM	_____
_____	5.PM	_____
_____	6.PM	_____
_____	7.PM	_____
_____	8.PM	_____
_____	9.PM	_____
_____	10.PM	_____
_____	11.PM	_____
_____	12.AM	_____

BREAKFAST

[ ]

LUNCH

[ ]

DINNER

[ ]

WATER

🥛 🥛 🥛 🥛 🥛
🥛 🥛 🥛 🥛 🥛

HAPPY SCALE

😀 🙂 😐 🙁 ☹️

MY REWARD

[ ]

DAILY PLANNER

TODAY IS /

WEATHER

TODAY I AM EXCITED ABOUT

TODAY I AM GRATEFUL FOR

TODAY'S TOP PRIORITY

1. _____
2. _____
3. _____

TO DO LIST

_____
_____
_____
_____
_____
_____
_____
_____
_____
_____

TODAY'S SCHEDULE

PLAN		TRACK
_____	5.AM	_____
_____	6.AM	_____
_____	7.AM	_____
_____	8.AM	_____
_____	9.AM	_____
_____	10.AM	_____
_____	11.AM	_____
_____	12.PM	_____
_____	1.PM	_____
_____	3.PM	_____
_____	4.PM	_____
_____	5.PM	_____
_____	6.PM	_____
_____	7.PM	_____
_____	8.PM	_____
_____	9.PM	_____
_____	10.PM	_____
_____	11.PM	_____
_____	12.AM	_____

BREAKFAST

LUNCH

DINNER

WATER

HAPPY SCALE

😀 🙂 😐 🙁 😫

MY REWARD

DAILY PLANNER

🗓 TODAY IS /

WEATHER

TODAY I AM EXCITED ABOUT

TODAY I AM GRATEFUL FOR

TODAY'S TOP PRIORITY

1. _____
2. _____
3. _____

TO DO LIST

_____
_____
_____
_____
_____
_____
_____
_____
_____
_____

TODAY'S SCHEDULE

PLAN		TRACK
_____	5.AM	_____
_____	6.AM	_____
_____	7.AM	_____
_____	8.AM	_____
_____	9.AM	_____
_____	10.AM	_____
_____	11.AM	_____
_____	12.PM	_____
_____	1.PM	_____
_____	3.PM	_____
_____	4.PM	_____
_____	5.PM	_____
_____	6.PM	_____
_____	7.PM	_____
_____	8.PM	_____
_____	9.PM	_____
_____	10.PM	_____
_____	11.PM	_____
_____	12.AM	_____

BREAKFAST

LUNCH

DINNER

WATER

HAPPY SCALE

😀 🙂 😐 🙁 😫

MY REWARD

DAILY PLANNER

TODAY IS /

WEATHER

TODAY I AM EXCITED ABOUT

TODAY I AM GRATEFUL FOR

TODAY'S TOP PRIORITY

1.
2.
3.

TO DO LIST

TODAY'S SCHEDULE

PLAN		TRACK
	5.AM	
	6.AM	
	7.AM	
	8.AM	
	9.AM	
	10.AM	
	11.AM	
	12.PM	
	1.PM	
	3.PM	
	4.PM	
	5.PM	
	6.PM	
	7.PM	
	8.PM	
	9.PM	
	10.PM	
	11.PM	
	12.AM	

BREAKFAST

LUNCH

DINNER

WATER

HAPPY SCALE

😀   🙂   😐   🙁   😩

MY REWARD

DAILY PLANNER

📅 TODAY IS /

WEATHER

TODAY I AM EXCITED ABOUT

TODAY I AM GRATEFUL FOR

TODAY'S TOP PRIORITY

1. _____
2. _____
3. _____

TO DO LIST

_____
_____
_____
_____
_____
_____
_____
_____

TODAY'S SCHEDULE

PLAN		TRACK
_____	5.AM	_____
_____	6.AM	_____
_____	7.AM	_____
_____	8.AM	_____
_____	9.AM	_____
_____	10.AM	_____
_____	11.AM	_____
_____	12.PM	_____
_____	1.PM	_____
_____	3.PM	_____
_____	4.PM	_____
_____	5.PM	_____
_____	6.PM	_____
_____	7.PM	_____
_____	8.PM	_____
_____	9.PM	_____
_____	10.PM	_____
_____	11.PM	_____
_____	12.AM	

BREAKFAST

LUNCH

DINNER

WATER

HAPPY SCALE

MY REWARD

DAILY PLANNER

📅 TODAY IS /

WEATHER

TODAY I AM EXCITED ABOUT

TODAY I AM GRATEFUL FOR

TODAY'S TOP PRIORITY

1. _____
2. _____
3. _____

TO DO LIST

_____
_____
_____
_____
_____
_____
_____
_____
_____
_____
_____

TODAY'S SCHEDULE

PLAN		TRACK
_____	5.AM	_____
_____	6.AM	_____
_____	7.AM	_____
_____	8.AM	_____
_____	9.AM	_____
_____	10.AM	_____
_____	11.AM	_____
_____	12.PM	_____
_____	1.PM	_____
_____	3.PM	_____
_____	4.PM	_____
_____	5.PM	_____
_____	6.PM	_____
_____	7.PM	_____
_____	8.PM	_____
_____	9.PM	_____
_____	10.PM	_____
_____	11.PM	_____
_____	12.AM	

BREAKFAST

LUNCH

DINNER

WATER

HAPPY SCALE

😀 🙂 😐 ☹️ 😫

MY REWARD

DAILY PLANNER

TODAY IS /

WEATHER

TODAY I AM EXCITED ABOUT

TODAY I AM GRATEFUL FOR

TODAY'S TOP PRIORITY

1. _____
2. _____
3. _____

TO DO LIST

_____
_____
_____
_____
_____
_____
_____
_____
_____
_____
_____
_____

TODAY'S SCHEDULE

PLAN		TRACK
_____	5.AM	_____
_____	6.AM	_____
_____	7.AM	_____
_____	8.AM	_____
_____	9.AM	_____
_____	10.AM	_____
_____	11.AM	_____
_____	12.PM	_____
_____	1.PM	_____
_____	3.PM	_____
_____	4.PM	_____
_____	5.PM	_____
_____	6.PM	_____
_____	7.PM	_____
_____	8.PM	_____
_____	9.PM	_____
_____	10.PM	_____
_____	11.PM	_____
_____	12.AM	_____

BREAKFAST

LUNCH

DINNER

WATER

HAPPY SCALE

MY REWARD

DAILY PLANNER

TODAY IS /

WEATHER

TODAY I AM EXCITED ABOUT

TODAY I AM GRATEFUL FOR

TODAY'S TOP PRIORITY

1. _____
2. _____
3. _____

TO DO LIST

_____
_____
_____
_____
_____
_____
_____
_____
_____
_____
_____

TODAY'S SCHEDULE

PLAN		TRACK
_____	5.AM	_____
_____	6.AM	_____
_____	7.AM	_____
_____	8.AM	_____
_____	9.AM	_____
_____	10.AM	_____
_____	11.AM	_____
_____	12.PM	_____
_____	1.PM	_____
_____	3.PM	_____
_____	4.PM	_____
_____	5.PM	_____
_____	6.PM	_____
_____	7.PM	_____
_____	8.PM	_____
_____	9.PM	_____
_____	10.PM	_____
_____	11.PM	_____
_____	12.AM	_____

BREAKFAST

LUNCH

DINNER

WATER

HAPPY SCALE

MY REWARD

DAILY PLANNER

📅 TODAY IS /

WEATHER

TODAY I AM EXCITED ABOUT

TODAY I AM GRATEFUL FOR

TODAY'S TOP PRIORITY

1. _____
2. _____
3. _____

TO DO LIST

_____
_____
_____
_____
_____
_____
_____
_____
_____
_____
_____
_____

TODAY'S SCHEDULE

PLAN		TRACK
_____	5.AM	_____
_____	6.AM	_____
_____	7.AM	_____
_____	8.AM	_____
_____	9.AM	_____
_____	10.AM	_____
_____	11.AM	_____
_____	12.PM	_____
_____	1.PM	_____
_____	3.PM	_____
_____	4.PM	_____
_____	5.PM	_____
_____	6.PM	_____
_____	7.PM	_____
_____	8.PM	_____
_____	9.PM	_____
_____	10.PM	_____
_____	11.PM	_____
_____	12.AM	_____

BREAKFAST

LUNCH

DINNER

WATER

HAPPY SCALE

MY REWARD

DAILY PLANNER

TODAY IS /

WEATHER

TODAY I AM EXCITED ABOUT

TODAY I AM GRATEFUL FOR

TODAY'S TOP PRIORITY

1. _____
2. _____
3. _____

TO DO LIST

_____
_____
_____
_____
_____
_____
_____
_____
_____
_____
_____

TODAY'S SCHEDULE

PLAN		TRACK
_____	5.AM	_____
_____	6.AM	_____
_____	7.AM	_____
_____	8.AM	_____
_____	9.AM	_____
_____	10.AM	_____
_____	11.AM	_____
_____	12.PM	_____
_____	1.PM	_____
_____	3.PM	_____
_____	4.PM	_____
_____	5.PM	_____
_____	6.PM	_____
_____	7.PM	_____
_____	8.PM	_____
_____	9.PM	_____
_____	10.PM	_____
_____	11.PM	_____
_____	12.AM	_____

BREAKFAST

LUNCH

DINNER

WATER

HAPPY SCALE

MY REWARD

DAILY PLANNER

TODAY IS /   WEATHER

TODAY I AM EXCITED ABOUT

TODAY I AM GRATEFUL FOR

TODAY'S TOP PRIORITY

1. _____
2. _____
3. _____

TO DO LIST

_____
_____
_____
_____
_____
_____
_____
_____
_____
_____

TODAY'S SCHEDULE

PLAN		TRACK
_____	5.AM	_____
_____	6.AM	_____
_____	7.AM	_____
_____	8.AM	_____
_____	9.AM	_____
_____	10.AM	_____
_____	11.AM	_____
_____	12.PM	_____
_____	1.PM	_____
_____	3.PM	_____
_____	4.PM	_____
_____	5.PM	_____
_____	6.PM	_____
_____	7.PM	_____
_____	8.PM	_____
_____	9.PM	_____
_____	10.PM	_____
_____	11.PM	_____
_____	12.AM	_____

BREAKFAST

LUNCH

DINNER

WATER

HAPPY SCALE

MY REWARD

DAILY PLANNER

📅 TODAY IS /

WEATHER

TODAY I AM EXCITED ABOUT

TODAY I AM GRATEFUL FOR

TODAY'S TOP PRIORITY

1. _____
2. _____
3. _____

TO DO LIST

_____
_____
_____
_____
_____
_____
_____
_____
_____
_____
_____
_____

TODAY'S SCHEDULE

PLAN		TRACK
_____	5.AM	_____
_____	6.AM	_____
_____	7.AM	_____
_____	8.AM	_____
_____	9.AM	_____
_____	10.AM	_____
_____	11.AM	_____
_____	12.PM	_____
_____	1.PM	_____
_____	3.PM	_____
_____	4.PM	_____
_____	5.PM	_____
_____	6.PM	_____
_____	7.PM	_____
_____	8.PM	_____
_____	9.PM	_____
_____	10.PM	_____
_____	11.PM	_____
_____	12.AM	_____

BREAKFAST

LUNCH

DINNER

WATER

HAPPY SCALE

😀 🙂 😐 🙁 ☹️

MY REWARD

DAILY PLANNER

TODAY IS /

WEATHER

TODAY I AM EXCITED ABOUT

TODAY I AM GRATEFUL FOR

TODAY'S TOP PRIORITY

1. _____
2. _____
3. _____

TO DO LIST

_____
_____
_____
_____
_____
_____
_____
_____
_____
_____
_____
_____
_____

TODAY'S SCHEDULE

PLAN		TRACK
_____	5.AM	_____
_____	6.AM	_____
_____	7.AM	_____
_____	8.AM	_____
_____	9.AM	_____
_____	10.AM	_____
_____	11.AM	_____
_____	12.PM	_____
_____	1.PM	_____
_____	3.PM	_____
_____	4.PM	_____
_____	5.PM	_____
_____	6.PM	_____
_____	7.PM	_____
_____	8.PM	_____
_____	9.PM	_____
_____	10.PM	_____
_____	11.PM	_____
_____	12.AM	_____

BREAKFAST

LUNCH

DINNER

WATER

HAPPY SCALE

MY REWARD

DAILY PLANNER

TODAY IS /

WEATHER

TODAY I AM EXCITED ABOUT

TODAY I AM GRATEFUL FOR

TODAY'S TOP PRIORITY

1. _____
2. _____
3. _____

TO DO LIST

_____
_____
_____
_____
_____
_____
_____
_____
_____
_____

TODAY'S SCHEDULE

PLAN		TRACK
_____	5.AM	_____
_____	6.AM	_____
_____	7.AM	_____
_____	8.AM	_____
_____	9.AM	_____
_____	10.AM	_____
_____	11.AM	_____
_____	12.PM	_____
_____	1.PM	_____
_____	3.PM	_____
_____	4.PM	_____
_____	5.PM	_____
_____	6.PM	_____
_____	7.PM	_____
_____	8.PM	_____
_____	9.PM	_____
_____	10.PM	_____
_____	11.PM	_____
_____	12.AM	_____

BREAKFAST

LUNCH

DINNER

WATER

HAPPY SCALE

MY REWARD

DAILY PLANNER

🗓 TODAY IS /

WEATHER

TODAY I AM EXCITED ABOUT

TODAY I AM GRATEFUL FOR

TODAY'S TOP PRIORITY

1. _____
2. _____
3. _____

TO DO LIST

_____
_____
_____
_____
_____
_____
_____
_____
_____
_____
_____

TODAY'S SCHEDULE

PLAN		TRACK
_____	5.AM	_____
_____	6.AM	_____
_____	7.AM	_____
_____	8.AM	_____
_____	9.AM	_____
_____	10.AM	_____
_____	11.AM	_____
_____	12.PM	_____
_____	1.PM	_____
_____	3.PM	_____
_____	4.PM	_____
_____	5.PM	_____
_____	6.PM	_____
_____	7.PM	_____
_____	8.PM	_____
_____	9.PM	_____
_____	10.PM	_____
_____	11.PM	_____
_____	12.AM	_____

BREAKFAST

LUNCH

DINNER

WATER

HAPPY SCALE

😃 🙂 😐 🙁 ☹️

MY REWARD

DAILY PLANNER

📅 TODAY IS /

WEATHER ☀️ ⛅ 🌧️ 🌬️ ☀️

TODAY I AM EXCITED ABOUT

TODAY I AM GRATEFUL FOR

TODAY'S TOP PRIORITY

1. _____
2. _____
3. _____

TO DO LIST

_____
_____
_____
_____
_____
_____
_____
_____
_____
_____

TODAY'S SCHEDULE

PLAN		TRACK
_____	5.AM	_____
_____	6.AM	_____
_____	7.AM	_____
_____	8.AM	_____
_____	9.AM	_____
_____	10.AM	_____
_____	11.AM	_____
_____	12.PM	_____
_____	1.PM	_____
_____	3.PM	_____
_____	4.PM	_____
_____	5.PM	_____
_____	6.PM	_____
_____	7.PM	_____
_____	8.PM	_____
_____	9.PM	_____
_____	10.PM	_____
_____	11.PM	_____
_____	12.AM	_____

BREAKFAST

LUNCH

DINNER

WATER

🥤 🥤 🥤 🥤 🥤
🥤 🥤 🥤 🥤 🥤

HAPPY SCALE

😃 🙂 😐 🙁 😣

MY REWARD

DAILY PLANNER

📅 TODAY IS /

WEATHER

TODAY I AM EXCITED ABOUT

TODAY I AM GRATEFUL FOR

TODAY'S TOP PRIORITY

1. _____
2. _____
3. _____

TO DO LIST

_____
_____
_____
_____
_____
_____
_____
_____
_____
_____
_____
_____

TODAY'S SCHEDULE

PLAN		TRACK
_____	5.AM	_____
_____	6.AM	_____
_____	7.AM	_____
_____	8.AM	_____
_____	9.AM	_____
_____	10.AM	_____
_____	11.AM	_____
_____	12.PM	_____
_____	1.PM	_____
_____	3.PM	_____
_____	4.PM	_____
_____	5.PM	_____
_____	6.PM	_____
_____	7.PM	_____
_____	8.PM	_____
_____	9.PM	_____
_____	10.PM	_____
_____	11.PM	_____
_____	12.AM	_____

BREAKFAST

LUNCH

DINNER

WATER

🥛 🥛 🥛 🥛 🥛
🥛 🥛 🥛 🥛 🥛

HAPPY SCALE

MY REWARD

DAILY PLANNER

TODAY IS /

WEATHER

TODAY I AM EXCITED ABOUT

TODAY I AM GRATEFUL FOR

TODAY'S TOP PRIORITY

1.

2.

3.

TO DO LIST

TODAY'S SCHEDULE

PLAN		TRACK
	5.AM	
	6.AM	
	7.AM	
	8.AM	
	9.AM	
	10.AM	
	11.AM	
	12.PM	
	1.PM	
	3.PM	
	4.PM	
	5.PM	
	6.PM	
	7.PM	
	8.PM	
	9.PM	
	10.PM	
	11.PM	
	12.AM	

BREAKFAST

LUNCH

DINNER

WATER

HAPPY SCALE

MY REWARD

DAILY PLANNER

TODAY IS /   WEATHER

TODAY I AM EXCITED ABOUT

TODAY I AM GRATEFUL FOR

TODAY'S TOP PRIORITY

1. _____
2. _____
3. _____

TO DO LIST

_____
_____
_____
_____
_____
_____
_____
_____
_____
_____

TODAY'S SCHEDULE

PLAN		TRACK
_____	5.AM	_____
_____	6.AM	_____
_____	7.AM	_____
_____	8.AM	_____
_____	9.AM	_____
_____	10.AM	_____
_____	11.AM	_____
_____	12.PM	_____
_____	1.PM	_____
_____	3.PM	_____
_____	4.PM	_____
_____	5.PM	_____
_____	6.PM	_____
_____	7.PM	_____
_____	8.PM	_____
_____	9.PM	_____
_____	10.PM	_____
_____	11.PM	_____
_____	12.AM	_____

BREAKFAST   LUNCH

DINNER   WATER

HAPPY SCALE

MY REWARD

DAILY PLANNER

📅 TODAY IS /

WEATHER ☀️ ⛅ 🌧️ 🌬️ 🌞

TODAY I AM EXCITED ABOUT

TODAY I AM GRATEFUL FOR

TODAY'S TOP PRIORITY

1. _____
2. _____
3. _____

TO DO LIST

TODAY'S SCHEDULE

PLAN		TRACK
_____	5.AM	_____
_____	6.AM	_____
_____	7.AM	_____
_____	8.AM	_____
_____	9.AM	_____
_____	10.AM	_____
_____	11.AM	_____
_____	12.PM	_____
_____	1.PM	_____
_____	3.PM	_____
_____	4.PM	_____
_____	5.PM	_____
_____	6.PM	_____
_____	7.PM	_____
_____	8.PM	_____
_____	9.PM	_____
_____	10.PM	_____
_____	11.PM	_____
_____	12.AM	_____

BREAKFAST

LUNCH

DINNER

WATER

HAPPY SCALE

😃 🙂 😐 🙁 😫

MY REWARD

STAY CONNECTED

PUSH *power* BOSS

@PUSHPOWERBOSS

YouTube

PUSHPOWERBOSS@GMAIL.COM

www.ingramcontent.com/pod-product-compliance
Lightning Source LLC
Chambersburg PA
CBHW052341210326
41597CB00037B/6219